Prepaid College
Tuition Plans
Promise and Problems

Prepaid College Tuition Plans

Promise and Problems

Michael A. Olivas, editor
Professor of Law
Associate Dean for Research
Director, Institute for
Higher Education Law and Governance
University of Houston
Law Center

New York, College Entrance Examination Board, 1993

The College Board is a national nonprofit association that champions educational excellence for all students through the ongoing collaboration of more than 2,900 member schools, colleges, universities, educational systems, and associations. The Board promotes—by means of responsive forums, research, programs, and policy development—universal access to high standards of learning, equity of opportunity, and sufficient financial support so that every student is prepared for success in college and work.

In all of its publishing activities, the College Board endeavors to present the works of authors who are well qualified to write with authority on the subject at hand and to present accurate and timely information. However, the opinions, interpretations, and conclusions of the authors are their own and do not necessarily represent those of the College Board; nothing contained herein should be assumed to represent an official position of the College Board or any of its members.

Copies of this publication can be ordered from College Board Publications, Box 886, New York, NY 10101-0886. The price is $13.00.

Library of Congress Catalog Number: 92-075378

International Standard Book Number: 087447-484-1

Printed in the United States of America

Contents

Foreword

The College Board is very pleased to publish this volume on postsecondary prepaid tuition programs, conceived and edited by Professor Michael A. Olivas of the University of Houston Law Center. That the College Board publish *Prepaid College Tuition Plans: Promise and Problems* is appropriate for several reasons. First, the Board has played an important role in the debate over these programs' development (in 1987 and 1989), and second, by publishing the first collections of scholarship on this topic. The progress of scholarship on prepaid tuition programs closely parallels the development of the plans themselves. In 1987, the College Board cohosted an important symposium on the nascent plans then on the drawing board and subsequently published the conference proceedings. Two years later, the Board again cosponsored an invitational conference on the subject, and in 1990, published Janet Hansen's edited collection *(College Savings Plans: Public Policy Choices).*

The present volume brings to the topic the scholarship of legal scholars and public policy experts assessing the programs currently in place and gauging the successes and failures of state initiatives. The contributions are the result of a conference hosted not by the Board, but by a premier higher education research center, the University of Houston's Institute for Higher Education Law and Governance. These independently commissioned papers show rigorous and careful analytic work of the type traditionally promulgated over the years by the College Board in its various publications on financial aid and public policy. Although the Board did not create this forum, we are pleased to disseminate the findings.

One final College Board contribution is evident here: the work done by editor Michael A. Olivas. In addition to his many other scholarly duties, Professor Olivas has been, since 1990, a valuable Trustee of the College Board. As President, I have valued his advice and counsel and I am pleased to have this opportunity to share his scholarship with the larger research and policy community.

This collaboration has been a quintessential College Board undertaking, one that combines rigorous analysis with an overriding concern for equity. I recommend this work to all who have an interest in the financing of higher education.

Our thanks to the contributing authors, conference participants, and others, particularly Charlene Sullivan, Stephen Huber, Peter Roberts, Robert Mettlen, and Deborah Jones. Acknowledgments are also due Madelyn Roesch, editor at the College Board.

DONALD M. STEWART
PRESIDENT
THE COLLEGE BOARD

Chapter 1

Introduction:
Financing Higher Education

Michael A. Olivas

My admiration for those who administer TRIO and other student services, always high, was increased when I was asked to address an Upward Bound class in Madison, Wisconsin. The class was composed of a restless group of middle school students, all black, Hispanic, or Asian, on a Saturday afternoon when all of us would rather have been somewhere else. I gave a brief talk on what it takes to become a lawyer. As I have in dozens of such talks, I tried to stress how hard work and a sense of purpose are essential to any career, whether in law, teaching, music, or athletics. This prompted the usual questions about how much money lawyers made—a strong preoccupation among students—as well as how long it took to become an attorney. When I made a pitch to avoid using drugs, they perked up. Several reminded me that some attorneys defend drug dealers. When I noted that someone with a drug record might not be able to become a lawyer, one astute 13-year-old floored me with the question, "Is that juvis [juvenile records] or adult?" I was mortified, and while I considered myself pretty good on my feet and no prude, I was struck by how college-going for minorities and low-income kids is a much different world than college-going is for the affluent, even in predominantly white and prosperous Madison. Imagine how much more pronounced this disparity is in such areas as the Valley in Albuquerque, Watts in Los Angeles, the Fourth Ward in Houston, the West Side of Chicago, and the South Bronx in New York—where students' only contacts with attorneys are probably through their own or a family member's involvement with a public defender. It's little wonder that they aspire unrealistically to ca-

reers as NBA stars or rappers. Latino students have a better chance of
playing in major league baseball than of becoming law professors.

I relate this anecdote to indicate the difficulty of the task faced by
TRIO professionals and other student personnel workers, and to set the
context for an examination of financial aid practices, including prepaid
tuition programs. The legislation governing higher education finance is
extremely complex and difficult, and the simple policy objectives of delivering the most aid to the most deserving are not so simple in the exe-
cution. I find that National Public Radio (NPR) often helps me understand complex issues, and I adopt their way in this instance. To explain
complex events in Bosnia, or to gauge the effect of welfare reform in
Michigan, NPR uses a variety of devices: reporters will interview persons
affected by the event, will locate an articulate translator of the process, or
will use vignettes to elaborate the human dimension of the issue. They
routinely include those normally excluded voices, those of people of col-
or or others not always thought of as authoritative. Of course, their format as an alternative news medium allows them to spend more time on
the stories than does the talking-head or sound-byte format of commercial media. In my way, this introductory chapter attempts the NPR approach. After reviewing recent federal legislation concerning higher education, particularly efforts to reach low-income and minority families, I
concentrate on the most significant state development in funding higher
education, prepaid tuition programs.

THE NEED FOR INFORMATION

Reflections on the College-Going Process

Almost any need-based financial aid program will help minority students
in the postsecondary system. The problem is that financial aid and financial aid information are available only to those students already admitted
into an institution. Three dimensions of the financial aid delivery system
disproportionately discourage minority students, particularly blacks and
Hispanics, from seeking or achieving admission to colleges and universities: information inequities, negative consequences of system complexity,
and institutional aid practices. To some extent, these issues affect all students, but they affect minority students most directly and detrimentally
because of the poverty of many of these students, the structural features

of our higher education system, and the historical racism that has characterized higher education in the United States.

Information Inequities

Information inequities have a negative impact on minority communities, especially those that are bilingual; these groups often require less formal information systems than do majority populations. Studies of underparticipation in social service programs by extremely poor families have attributed the low rates to poorly designed information-delivery systems.[1]

These deficiencies in "getting the word out" crucially affect black and Hispanic populations. These students attend high schools where college aspirations are not the norm. It is likely that parents of minority students have not attended college and in the case of Hispanics, are unlikely to have graduated from high school. So these parents, even if they desire college for their children, are not enmeshed in the social networks or alumni recruiting efforts that college graduates enjoy. In many cases, the cost of college looms so large as to make it seem completely inaccessible for their children; the expense of attending college often exceeds the annual wages of many minority families.

Of course, many institutions try hard to recruit, but the most successful recruiting efforts are those that measure student "merit" by either high test scores or high athletic scores. National Merit Scholars and graceful seven-footers are likely to come to the attention of many colleges, and fierce, often shameless, competition ensues. In fact, the National Collegiate Athletic Association (NCAA) has had to fashion rules to *limit* recruiting for student athletes.

We know how to recruit. When institutions deem it important to attract certain students, they mobilize their resources and recruit as if their reputations demanded it. Once a school is effective in these pursuits and develops a reputation for supporting its high scorers, the information networks become more effective and far-reaching. Alumni and counselors assist; reputations are established and maintained. We've even solved "articulation problems" and coordinate the flow of athletes from junior colleges to senior programs. However, for the great mass of medium or low scorers, the word is simply not enough. I believe that institutions that want to recruit minority students can do so, but only with the same kind of long-term commitment and resources that are employed to establish information networks for attracting honors students and athletically talented students. Few institutions seem committed to such a coordinated information campaign for recruiting and providing aid to minority students, and the poor numbers show the results.[2]

System Complexity

The complexity of financial assistance programs, which poses problems even for middle-class families, renders such programs virtually inaccessible to poor families. Anyone who has completed an income tax return (and many low-income individuals are not required to do so) realizes the degree of reading and arithmetic skills necessary for completing the forms, even if a standard deduction is used. Completing the necessary financial aid forms is even more complex than completing tax returns and requires more calculation of assets. For poor families, who have few tangible assets, this is a nearly impossible task without assistance. Talent Search and other federal TRIO programs intended to assist disadvantaged students in these tasks are woefully underfunded, with no prospects of improvement. Furthermore, federal efforts to ferret out possible fraud have made completing the forms even more complicated.

In addition, few minority parents have the previous credit records with banks required to readily secure the information and assistance available for various kinds of loans. Despite the extraordinary profits guaranteed to the lending industry, banks have made little systematic effort to simplify paperwork or reach out to minority communities to encourage prudent student loans. In my view, the counseling provided by financial aid offices is pro forma and not very useful. How could it be otherwise, given the overworked staff on most campuses?

The most detrimental consequence of system complexity, however, is the most obvious: fewer poor people can afford college or its "start-up" costs. Application fees, test and transcript fees, form preparation expenses, and other related costs are incurred even before an application is complete and considered by a college. Some colleges allow or encourage videotaped applications from students, surely skewing the pool toward the advantaged. Poor families, even those who stumble upon available fee waivers, often lack the required sophistication for negotiating the high technology of college choice—assuming they even have a college in mind.

Institutional Aid Policies

Institutional aid policies themselves pose the biggest problem for minority students and the most formidable barrier to financial assistance. One recent study found that despite the low average income of the Hispanic families surveyed, only 48 percent applied for financial aid, and only 63 percent of those who applied received any aid award. If these findings are correct, it means that fewer than one-third of Hispanics requiring financial aid receive it.[3]

Another study, my own, uncovered an even more disturbing pattern: the extremely limited extent to which any financial aid packaging is aimed at Hispanics.[4] Over 60 percent of the Hispanic freshmen surveyed received only one source of aid (a Pell Grant); even when there was more than one source of aid, over 95 percent received Pell Grants. Since Pell Grants are the cornerstone of federal financial aid policy, it is reassuring to have evidence that Hispanics are receiving this assistance. However, 60 percent of Hispanic freshmen received only Pell Grants, and these grants covered only half of the cost of attendance. How are students making up the difference?

Alvin So, in a 1984 study, found that Hispanic parents, on average, received only 39 percent of the aid required to send their children to college.[5] Data reveal that need-based aid is delivering more assistance to needier families, but little additional *institutional* aid in the form of grants or scholarships is being awarded to Hispanics.[6] These findings reinforce the earlier point concerning institutional commitments: if institutions see minority students as "wards of the state" or as solely the government's responsibility, none of the discretionary aid used to attract high scorers (on academic tests or on the playing fields) will be used to improve minority attendance.

Another problem is the tendency of minority students and their parents to overreport annual income. In a recent study, I found that most Hispanic students simply did not know how much their parents earned, and that Hispanic parents erred substantially on the conservative side when called upon to complete aid forms.[7] Only 21 percent of Hispanic freshmen accurately reported family income within $500 (a significant amount when over 70 percent of the families earned less than $10,500 in 1979); most interestingly, 56 percent overestimated, while only 22 percent underestimated. The most impoverished (those whose family incomes were less than $7,500) were far more likely to overestimate (60 percent) than to underestimate (6 percent).[8]

The bulk of self-report literature and the increased federal reporting requirements, however, are concerned with documenting the tendency of families to "shelter" or not report income. This is a reasonable concern, to be sure, but a practice unlikely to occur in poor families, who have little to spend or shelter.[9] Federal or institutional policies that would require submission of the Internal Revenue Service Form 1040 as income verification, however, would disproportionately affect low-income persons, who often do not have either the resources or technical assistance to complete complex forms. Those in the lowest income brackets would be required to complete a 1040 form and verify eligibility even though they had no statutory requirement to file with the IRS.

The pronounced tendency of low-income families to overreport income does pose problems, though of a different sort than the problems imagined by those who have supported additional reporting requirements. For instance, overreporting income can lead to reduced eligibility and aid awards (because aid deadlines occur before IRS deadlines or the end of the calendar year, when a family knows how much it will have earned that year); this error would be compounded over the period of enrollment if it were not caught or corrected. In addition, many poor families, particularly in times of high unemployment, are unlikely to be able to document income with the required specificity. Persons who are not regularly employed (but may do piecework, housecleaning, odd jobs, day labor, or agricultural work), or whose employers do not keep regular or timely records will be unable to document income or assets. Lack of technical assistance in completing forms often results in late, incomplete, or inaccurate applications. Often, needy families will not fit computer profiles, and their aid will be denied or delayed. Immigrant families may be hesitant to interact with bureaucracies that require detailed personal information. Overextended aid offices are unlikely to offer adequate assistance; merely keeping up with the correct and timely forms often overwhelms even the best-run offices. Requirements that poverty be better documented are likely to discourage many families, particularly minority families, from applying for aid.

These problems should not be used to argue for the reduction of financial aid programs. That they do not work better is no reason to reduce or eliminate them. That they fail to ferret out all income fraud is no reason to impose paperwork requirements that will increase obstacles for low-income persons. Those minority students who do manage to negotiate the shoals seem to receive aid according to their need, at least if their self-help portion is not unreasonably high. On balance, the system works well for those who get into the system.

This hedged endorsement, however, does not spare institutions of higher education from sharp criticism. Tolerating poorly administered and understaffed financial aid offices is a false economy. Using discretionary institutional aid only to attract high scorers is a mistake, particularly as more and more institutions compete for these academic and athletic blue-chippers. Most important, however, institutions themselves brought on the proposed reduction and Pell Grant cutbacks, by successfully inducing Congress to legislate the Middle Income Student Assistance Act (MISAA) of 1978. MISAA set off a round of tuition increases, played the wealthy off against the poor, and hastened the transfer of college costs from parents to the government. In this and other areas, higher education has been a victim of its own excesses. Colleges must commit themselves to work for future aid policies that deliver the highest proportion of aid, with maximum accessibility and minimum red tape, to the low-income students who need it most. To do less will exclude these students, many of them very bright and capable.

STATE PREPAID TUITION PLANS
AND EDUCATION SAVINGS PLANS

In contrast to the longstanding traditions of loans, grants, and scholarships, state financing of higher education by prepaid tuition plans is more recent. Although Michigan was the first state to enact legislation for such a plan, Wyoming actually sold the first contract in 1986. As of December 1992, six states (Alabama, Alaska, Florida, Michigan, Ohio, and Wyoming) have formal prepaid programs; Pennsylvania has enabling legislation on the books and is seeking vendors for a 1993 start-up. Kentucky has a hybrid education savings account program with an endowment component. (The Michigan Education Trust, MET, program is on hold, due to extensive public criticism and an adverse tax determination. See Chapters 3 and 5.) The states that currently have prepaid tuition programs with guaranteed tuition components are listed in Table 1.1. Florida's Prepaid Postsecondary Education Expense Program is the clear frontrunner; in four years it has sold nearly 200,000 contracts.

Table 1.1. State Prepaid Tuition Programs

Wallace-Folsum Prepaid College Tuition Trust Fund: Alabama Code §16-33C-3 (1991).

Alaska Education Trust Fund: Alaska Stat. 014.40.8 §3 (1991).

Florida Prepaid Postsecondary Education Expense Program: Florida Stat. Ann. §240.551 (West 1989 and Supp. 1992).

The Baccalaureate Education System Trust: Indiana Code Ann. §21-8-3 (Burns 1991).* **

Kentucky Educational Savings Plan Trust: Kentucky Rev. Stat. Ann. §164A.300 164.380.††

Louisiana Education Tuition Trust and Savings Plan Fund: Louisiana Rev. Stat. Ann. §17:3129 (West 1989 and Supp. 1992).†

Student Educational Enhancement Deposit Act: Maine Rev. Stat. Ann. tit. 20A §12601 (West 1990). (Repealed 1991).*

Michigan Education Trust Act: Michigan Comp. Laws Ann. §3900.1444 (West 1988).*

Missouri Access to Higher Education Act: Missouri Ann. Stat. §166.200 (Vernon's 1991).†

College Savings Program: Ohio Rev. Code Ann. §3334.02 (Anderson 1990).

Oklahoma Tuition Trust Act: Oklahoma Stat. tit. 70, §6002 (West 1989).†

Tuition Account Program and College Savings Bond Act: 1992 Pennsylvania Legis. Serv. 176 (Purdon).†

Baccalaureate Education System Trust: Tennessee Code Ann. §49-7-801 (1987). (Repealed 1989).*

West Virginia Higher Education Tuition Trust Act: West Virginia Code §18-30-2 (1988).†

Advance Payment of Higher Education Costs: Wyoming Stat. §21-16-501 (1991).

---

* Inactive or suspended operation.
† Not yet operational.
** Several state institutions administer their own programs.
†† Combined prepaid tuition fund and savings plan trust.

Many more states have moved to enact education savings plans, either through stand-alone bond issues or by earmarking a portion of larger, general obligation bond issues. To list these plans is difficult, because several states with statutory authority (e.g., Louisiana) issued more than one set of education bonds, and others (e.g., Indiana and Minnesota) never promulgated regulations or developed full-fledged programs. Maine repealed its enabling legislation. In contrast, Connecticut has become the Florida of education bond programs, issuing general obligation bonds every six months for the last five years—totaling nearly one billion dollars. In Indiana, individual public institutions issued their own bonds. The states that currently have education savings plans are listed in Table 1.2.

Although virtually all of the states with bond programs have "Education," "College," or "Trustee" in their statutory language, bond purchasers need not necessarily use the proceeds for college expenses. For example, although Connecticut refuses to sell bonds to institutional purchasers, private individuals who purchase the bonds are not required to spend the money on higher education; they need not have college-age beneficiaries; and they need not reside in the state. Some states allow institutional investors to purchase bonds in large quantities for investment portfolio purposes, while other states have engaged in more commercial, consumer-oriented programs. Connecticut is the premier example, with an 800-phone number, over 60 outlets for purchasing bonds, and a sophisticated and extensive public-relations and marketing program: every school child and licensed motorist in the state receives bond sale notices.

When one totals these programs and adds the Federal Series EE Bonds and private-sector initiatives (e.g., the College Savings Bank of Princeton, New Jersey; see Chapter 5), it is incontestable that many means for financing higher education exist outside the traditional federal assistance programs of the Higher Education Act, Title IV.

The avowed aim of some of these plans appears to be a stimulation of parental saving for their children's education. According to Janet S. Hansen, whose careful scholarship on federal financial aid issues has made her an authority on this topic:

> One of the major current disagreements among economists [over whether governments should enact policies to increase families' saving for college] has to do with the nation's declining rate of saving and whether past efforts to encourage saving did much to change behavior. There is little consensus about whether financial incentives encourage

Table 1.2. College Tuition Assistance Programs and Savings Bond Programs

Arkansas College Savings General Obligation Bond*

California Savings Bond Program*

Connecticut College Savings Bond Program*

Delaware*

Hawaii*

Illinois College Savings Bonds*

Indiana College Savings Bonds*

Iowa College Super Savings Plan*

Kentucky Educational Savings Plan Trust Act†

Louisiana Education Tuition and Savings Plan**

Maine Student Educational Enhancement Deposit Plan††

Michigan Education Trust††

Minnesota††

Missouri College Savings Bond**

New Hampshire College Savings Bonds*

North Carolina Capital Appreciation Bond Program*

North Dakota Educational Bonds for Savings Program*

Ohio College Savings Program**

Oregon Baccalaureate Bond Program*

Rhode Island College and University Savings Bond Program*

South Dakota Education Savings Program*

Tennessee Baccalaureate Education Savings Program*

Texas College Savings Bond Program*

Virginia Tuition Savings Program*

Washington College Savings Bond Program*

Wisconsin Higher Education Bond Program*

---

* Savings bonds or earmarked general obligation bonds.
† Combined trust fund and prepaid endowment fund.
** Combined education savings program and guaranteed tuition plan.
†† Inactive or suspended operation.

increased saving or only cause savers to shift their funds from one kind of saving instrument to another. The 1980s saw high real interest rates, lower tax rates on income, and special incentives for saving—in sum, a very positive climate for savers. Yet the personal savings rate dropped. This history should make policymakers cautious about thinking that they can dramatically affect family behavior by adding this or that feature to a college savings plan.[10]

Hansen wrote this at a time when the real estate market was booming, the stock market was at historic levels, rates of return on savings were high, and capital gains taxes had been lowered. The political ramifications become more sharply defined in hard financial times, both at the federal level and in state-based programs. Moreover, the generally bleak economic situation exacerbates families' need for information. If poor communities already lack consumer information and fear the cost of college for their children, news stories about rising college prices and a dynamic marketplace of subsidized financing options will likely increase the gap in college attendance between the poor and the wealthy.

SCOPE OF THIS VOLUME

Paul Horvitz, a leading finance scholar, considers the psychology of savings programs, as well as the more traditional financial and political issues. Chapter 2 clearly sets out the competing financial theories at play in this field, weighing each for its equity and efficiency. After balancing the effects of various state proposals, he concludes that the true rationale for prepaid tuition plans is the maintenance of relatively low tuition levels, and that such low levels favor the wealthy—who are disproportionately more likely to attend college and consume the benefit. He finds this rationale to be a "weak reed on which to base a major government program."

In Chapter 3, Jeffrey Lehman, one of the early and most prominent scholars in the area of prepaid tuition plans, follows up his influential 1990 *Michigan Law Review* article, "Social Irresponsibility, Actuarial Assumptions, and Wealth Redistribution: Lessons About Public Policy from a Prepaid Tuition Program," with a careful study of MET's decision to expand its subscriber base by offering a monthly payment option (MPO). In his 1990 article, Lehman charted the redistribution of state subsidy benefits upward to the most-advantaged Michigan residents. In 1990, partially in reaction to this criticism, the MET board changed its way of

selling contracts to allow purchasers to spread out the payments over a period of time. It was anticipated that this would permit families with lower
incomes to participate, especially since the size of monthly payments is
often more salient to low-income consumers than is the total obligation.

Lehman's data show that the availability of monthly options reduced
the "skewedness" of the original MET purchaser profiles, but not by a
substantial margin, and measurement discrepancies between the periods
before and after the change make comparisons difficult. To counter this
distributional effect, Lehman suggests a sliding-scale price approach, pre-
sumably a means-tested methodology that would not more heavily subsidize the wealthier purchasers. Of course, the federal mechanism for sliding-scale parental contributions is itself a political act, caught in a tug of
war between Congress and the Secretary of Education; its theoretical sim-
plicity predictably bogs down in the political details. For example, something such as treatment of home equity or farm ownership can make an
extraordinary difference in federal financial aid eligibility.[11] At the state
level, I suggested several years ago that states consider sliding-scale subsidization based on state residency, but this dog has not hunted.[12]

In Chapter 4, William Montjoy, an attorney who directs the successful Florida program, counters the more critical analysis offered by Professor Lehman and other researchers. Florida has avoided many of the administrative and political problems that Michigan has faced or created in
its MET program, such as not discounting its contracts. Indeed, Montjoy
concedes that it may be possible and appropriate to charge higher
amounts for the contracts. This feature could dovetail with Lehman's sliding-scale proposal—based on purchasers' income, their own college attendance history (favoring children whose parents did not attend college), or
other criteria. Montjoy acknowledges that the purpose of a plan is to
stimulate saving, and he is certainly correct when he argues that public
confidence in the plan's efficacy is essential. He does not add that being in
a state with a booming population helps, although it appears clear that
Florida's demographic and actuarial statistics are better than those of in-
dustrial-belt Michigan in this context.

David Williams II, a leading tax scholar, has carefully reviewed the
tax consequences of college savings plans. Chapter 5 presents the first
published scholarship on the 1992 tax ruling case in Michigan, which was
the coup de grace for the MET program unless it is substantially over-
hauled. Although the tax consequences of all postsecondary plans are con-

siderable, they differ greatly in the details and family circumstances of the purchasers. Williams' work clearly sets out these details and persuasively argues that parents should consider investing in a variety of the available options.

Chapter 6 is the most technical in the book, but its analysis is easily the most crucial to the success of prepaid tuition programs. Unless the states are politically willing, within the tax laws, to underwrite any short-falls, these programs have to stand on their own, operating out of their own pooled resources. Of course, this means finding investment strategies whose returns approximate or better the college costs of the future. As Lewis Spellman shows, real total returns on long-term government debt instruments were lower than the tuition inflation rate in two-thirds of the years between 1966 and 1987, and this in a time of substantial economic growth in the country.

As Spellman notes, this uneven performance is due to (1) the pattern of college tuition increases, which have averaged nearly 3 percent more each year than the Consumer Price Index (for 1992-93, the College Board price figures were seen as newsworthy because the increases of 6 to 10 percent were "not as large as expected"),[13] and (2) the tendency of trust portfolios to invest in "safe" government debt instruments tied to long-term rates. Recent low interest rates and rising college costs—even if they are increasing at a lower rate than expected—could spell obvious disaster for guaranteed tuition plans. Like Paul Horvitz, who considers the psychological effects on parents or other purchasers investing in college contracts, Spellman sees psychological resistance by traditional government investor agencies and communities (which may have lucrative arrangements under the current investing regimes), and a psychological dimension, what he calls a "reputational capital" feature, in the market. Notwithstanding his pessimistic assessment of current investment behavior, he sees a silver lining in the clouds, noting that the time is ripe for inflation-adjusted finance mechanisms, because inflation is not currently a serious problem.

The following chapters provide a substantial contribution to the debate over the equity and efficiency of prepaid tuition plans, and an advance over the first generation of scholarship in this important area. Although the first articles on the topic are of recent vintage, appearing only five or six years ago, everyone knows more now. In addition to the increasing scholarship (and its growing interdisciplinary sophistication), there are hundreds of thousands of contracts being purchased and executed for beneficiary students. Prepaid plans, both public and private, have earned a place in the investment portfolios of parents, and it is safe to say that such plans will increase and prosper if they earn the trust of parent-investors and legislators. The failed MET experiment may be salvaged, and a reconstituted program could well appear. Its greatest legacy may turn out to be its innovation and precocity; even its mistakes showed others how to proceed in a bold legislative laboratory.

NOTES

1. For an extended review of these studies, see Michael A. Olivas, "Information Access Inequities: A Fatal Flaw in Education Voucher Plans," *Journal of Law and Education* 10 (1982): 441-465.

2. As an example, federal data show that Hispanic students constitute approximately 5 percent of U.S. college enrollments, despite the fact that they represent a much higher percentage of the total college-age youth population. See generally Michael A. Olivas, *Latino College Students* (New York: Teachers College Press, 1986). For an excellent study of blacks in higher education, see Lorenzo Morris, *Elusive Equality* (Washington, D.C.: Howard University Press, 1979).

3. Alvin So, "The Financing of College Education by Hispanic Parents," *Urban Education* 19 (1984): 145-160.

4. Michael A. Olivas, "Financial Aid Packaging Policies: Access and Ideology," *Journal of Higher Education* 56 (1985): 462-475.

5. So, "Hispanic Parents," Table 1.

6. Olivas, "Packaging Policies," 470-471.

7. Michael A. Olivas, "Financial Aid and Student Self-Reports: The Importance of Being Earnest," *Research in Higher Education* 29 (1986): 245-252.

8. Ibid., 251-252.

9. See Douglas Windham, "Federal Financial Aid Policy: The Case of the Pell Grant Quality Control Study," *Review of Higher Education* 4 (1984): 397-410. Windham has carefully investigated the purported evidence of widespread fraud and found most of the "abuses" to be nonexistent or minor. He concludes that the government's campaign in this area was a smoke screen for rolling back aid limits.

10. Janet S. Hansen, ed., *College Savings Plans: Public Policy Choices* (New York: College Entrance Examination Board, 1990), 4.

11. See generally Joseph Cronin and Sylvia Simmons, eds., *Student Loans, Risks and Realities* (Dover, Mass.: Auburn House, 1987); Lawrence E. Gladieux, ed., *Radical Reform or Incremental Change? Student Loan Policy Alternatives for the Federal Govern-*

ment (New York: College Entrance Examination Board, 1989). For educational finance comparative studies, see Maureen Woodhall, *Student Loans as a Means of Financing Higher Education: Lessons from International Experience* (Washington, D.C.: World Bank Staff Working Papers, No. 599, 1983); D. Bruce Johnstone, *Sharing the Costs of Higher Education* (New York: College Entrance Examination Board, 1986).

12. Michael A. Olivas, "Administering Intentions: Law, Theory, and Practice in Postsecondary Residency Requirements," *Journal of Higher Education* 59 (1988): 263-290.

13. College Board, "College Board Survey Finds College Tuition and Fees Rose 6 to 10 Percent on Average, for 1992-93, Increases Not as Large as Expected," *News from the College Board,* October 1992. See also *Trends in Student Aid: 1982 to 1992* (Washington, D.C.: College Entrance Examination Board, September 1992).

Chapter 2

Prepaid Tuition Plans:
An Exercise in Finance,
Psychology, and Politics

Paul M. Horvitz

The first prepaid tuition plan I ever heard of was the Duquesne plan. At the time, I thought of it as a clever device by which a university could obtain funds from dedicated alumni who were dead certain they wanted their children to go to Duquesne, and who were willing to make, in effect, a contribution to their alma mater if the children went elsewhere. Alternatively, they could view it as a contribution that might have a windfall payoff if the children did go to Duquesne. I never thought it would have wide appeal, but it involved private contracts between consenting adults, and that is their business.

Prepaid tuition plans sponsored by state governments are an entirely different matter, raising quite different issues. If they involve a subsidy of some sort, that affects all taxpayers in the state and raises questions about the distribution of the subsidy. And if a subsidy is *not* involved, why can't the development of such plans be left to the private sector? The private financial markets have been amazingly innovative in recent years in designing new financial products and contracts to meet economic needs. This has been particularly so when the need is for managing risk. I would not have predicted that there would be much interest in this device among

Paul M. Horvitz is Judge James A. Elkins Professor of Banking and Finance at the University of Houston.

parents. I have been surprised at the substantial volume of sales achieved in Michigan and Florida. I am still skeptical, but their success, as measured by sales, cannot be denied.

GOVERNMENTAL ACTION

Federal, state, and local governments have traditionally promoted education. All states provide free elementary and secondary education and operate and subsidize colleges and universities, although there are differences in the degree of subsidization. These differences are important in understanding the appeal of prepaid tuition plans.

At the federal level, we have both loan guaranteed programs and a government agency to make a secondary market in such loans (the Student Loan Marketing Association or Sallie Mae). There is a U.S. Savings bond instrument with tax benefits when used for college expenses, and there are proposals for an instrument similar to an individual retirement account (IRA) to provide a tax-deductible means of saving for this purpose. The justifications for these programs are that, in economic jargon, education is a public good, which involves externalities. That is, education benefits not only the person receiving it, but also the rest of society. Without government support, private spending on education would be based only on consideration of the private benefits, and hence there would be under-investment in education. I can also see a legitimate public interest if a state tries to retain its most educated citizens by providing educational opportunities within the state.

From the consumer's standpoint, education is one of the largest expenses to be faced during one's lifetime. There are other large expenses incurred over the typical life cycle, such as buying a home, medical expenses, and retirement. All three of these are the subjects of major government programs and large subsidies. All of these programs and subsidies have been criticized from time to time on grounds of efficiency or equity.

I am not going to analyze all of these programs, but I can cite examples of some of the subsidies. Government programs to promote and facilitate home ownership include tax deductibility of mortgage interest and real estate taxes, subsidization of savings and loans institutions (created for mortgage lending), government insurance of mortgages (VA and FHA), sponsorship of agencies to promote the secondary mortgage market (FNMA, GNMA, FHLMC), and the exclusion of the value of services of home ownership from income taxation. Retirement financing has been assisted by the tax treatment of IRAs and corporate pension contributions and, of course, by the Social Security system. Financing medical care is now a hot political topic, but we already have substantial government involvement through Medicare, the tax exemption for employer contributions for health insurance, and the tax deduction for medical expenses.

These items have in common the fact that they involve potentially large expenditures that cannot be handled out of current income. While it is not clear that there are market failures that require government involvement, these programs are so widespread that clearly the public believes these are areas deserving of government promotion to achieve desired social goals.

Without belaboring this issue any further, I think the evidence is convincing, even to one with decidedly free-market predilections, that promoting college education, and facilitating the ability of consumers to meet the costs of college education, are appropriate governmental activities. I am skeptical of the benefits of state-sponsored prepaid tuition plans, but not because I challenge the legitimacy of concern by state governments with this issue.

PROBLEMS ENCOUNTERED BY STUDENTS AND THEIR FAMILIES

Much of the literature about prepaid tuition plans is not precise about the problems such plans are attempting to address. There is, in fact, confusion of several quite different problems of college-cost affordability: (1) most important is the economic problem—a family may not have the resources necessary to cover the cost of a college education; (2) the financial problem—a family that has sufficient resources over time, and saves to prepare for future tuition needs, may find that tuition rates increase faster than the accumulated savings; and (3) the psychological problem—students and their parents may undergo many years of worrying about meeting college costs.

The Economic Problem

The solution to the economic problem is the subsidization of college costs through financial aid. There are many families whose economic resources over the period from the birth of a child to high school graduation are not going to be sufficient to cover the full costs of a college education. Prepaid tuition plans cannot solve the problem of the student who simply cannot afford college. While this is obvious, it should be stressed. More important, I think there is general agreement that any social resources devoted to prepaid tuition plans should not come at the expense of traditional financial aid programs aimed at this economic problem.

The Financial Problem

Prepaid tuition programs are aimed at the financial problem, which incorporates risk considerations. We know that college costs are high relative to average current income, and that they will be higher, in nominal dollars, in the future. Many analyses of the effect of inflation on future tuition rates seem to ignore that fact that salaries also rise with inflation. Most people (though certainly not all) with school-age children will find that their incomes will be higher when the children are ready for college.

We know what tuition increases have been in the past. One time-series shows an average rate of tuition increase of 5.8 percent since 1904, and the rate of increase since 1970 has been 10 percent.[1] We have some basis for projecting increases into the future. Since the largest part of college operating costs is labor costs, and since it seems unlikely that productivity increases on college campuses will keep up with productivity increases in the rest of the economy, it is almost inevitable that in the long run, tuition costs will increase at a somewhat faster rate than inflation generally. The obvious ways of increasing productivity, as measured by student credit hours per faculty member, involve measures associated with decreases in the quality of education—larger class sizes, heavier teaching loads for faculty, or greater use of telecommunications. A prediction that college tuition, on the average, will increase at a rate 2 or 3 percent over the rate of inflation over the next 15 or 20 years will not be far wrong. Of course, I cannot predict the rate of inflation very accurately, but that is not too serious a problem, because investment returns over time will also be affected by the inflation rate. Rates of return on money market funds, government and corporate bonds, and common stocks will reflect changes in the overall price level. We know from very long experience what we can expect of the long-term performance of these assets relative to the inflation rate. There is very little chance, based on the historical record, that tuition will increase in the future at a long-run rate *greatly* in excess of that which can be earned on a reasonably diversified investment portfolio.

This suggests an easy solution to the financial problem for those families with sufficient income and resources: save for future college costs starting far in advance and invest in the vehicle most compatible with attitudes toward risk. Equities have the best long-term record of exceeding the inflation rate, but with considerable year-to-year variability; short-term securities involve less risk, but lower returns.

Unfortunately, this does not solve the problem many people are worried about. Even finance professionals, who are very familiar with the historical record of investment performance, still worry. Their fear is that they may do all the right things—save an appropriate amount and invest in the right vehicle—but find at that crucial September that the stock market is down, or that tuition has increased at an astronomical rate for the past 10 years.

The Psychological Problem

Beyond the problem of risk is the problem of perception. This creates a *psychological* problem in that the student and his family may undergo years of worrying about economic and financial problems. According to Donald Stewart, president of the College Board, "fear of being unable to pay college costs is as bad as the fact—worse, actually,...if concern over costs makes [students] opt out of the college-going track early on."[2]

The psychological problem is a real one. In Chapter 4, William Montjoy, director of the Florida Prepaid Postsecondary Education Expense Board, notes that the Florida plan is aimed at the perception problem among middle-income Americans that "tuitions are going out of sight." Since these families may also see themselves as squeezed out of student aid/loan programs, the prepaid tuition approach may provide an incentive to saving and may prevent the opting out of the college track referred to above by Stewart. Montjoy reports that 63 percent of the participants in the Florida program had no savings plans for college expenses before enrolling in the program. The existence of a prepaid tuition plan may encourage families that have the economic resources to save sufficient sums to cover college costs to actually do so.

It may be helpful to compare perceptions of college costs with those of the other major expenditures I discussed earlier—home-buying, medical expenses, and retirement. When people buy a house, they typically finance the purchase with a long-term mortgage. They usually have a choice between a fixed-rate and an adjustable-rate mortgage. Most people seem to have a strong preference for the obligation fixed in nominal terms—they seek to avoid the risk of an unexpected change in their monthly dollar obligations. An adjustable-rate mortgage involves only modest risk, and the government has imposed a number of regulations designed to protect the borrower in such transactions, but consumers prefer to avoid that risk.

The degree of risk in retirement planning is very much greater, and the government has assumed a much greater role in dealing with this risk. The Social Security system provides a basic retirement income, with benefits adjusted for inflation.

The financing of medical care is currently the most controversial of these issues. Interestingly, the discussion involves the same confusion that exists about tuition: whether the problem is one of the level of expected expenses or of the risk. For most of the elderly, Medicare, supplemented by private ("Medigap") insurance, is the solution. Most employed individuals can afford the cost of privately-available, actuarially-fair medical insurance. Much of the debate is about the level of subsidy of these premiums—either by the government or by one's employer. Some debate concerns those who cannot afford an actuarially-fair premium because of a preexisting condition. This latter group faces what I have called the economic problem. But as in the tuition situation, many find that while they can afford costs at current levels, the rate of increase of medical costs is frightening; this fear is analogous to the financial and psychological problems that affect tuition costs.

The Extent of Risk

As I have noted, the risk that a family prudently saving and investing will come up short of meeting future tuition costs does not seem to indicate a major problem. That is, the family that estimates its future needs at $120,000 and accumulates that amount may indeed find that costs turn out to be $130,000 or $140,000. On a comparative basis, a shortfall of $10,000 is modest compared to the needs of many. Of course, if costs turned out to be $200,000, that might well pose a serious problem, but there is little evidence to suggest that as a realistic possibility. Arthur Hauptman of the American Council on Education says, "the real risk to the family ... is that they would put money aside for savings and the money is not going to keep up or stay close to tuition...[T] his risk is not all that large and ... the fear is really greater than the reality."[3]

ELIMINATION OF RISK

Whatever the probability of that bad outcome, it is one that prepayment plans eliminate (though most such plans introduce new and different risks). Some plans—Duquesne, Michigan, and Florida—seem popular in part because they are underpriced or involve some subsidy. The extent to which such subsidies are necessary or appropriate will be discussed later, but first I want to focus on the risk-elimination aspect of the plans.

There are two questions that strike me as crucial to this discussion of state-sponsored plans:

1. Are consumers willing to pay to eliminate this risk?
2. If there is a demand for such risk minimization, can the private sector provide it?

The experience of Michigan and Florida seems to suggest that the answer to the first question is "yes," although it is not clear how much people are willing to pay. And it will probably be the wealthy who are willing to pay to eliminate the worry that goes along with financial risk.

With regard to the second question, there are various ways in which the private sector could reduce or eliminate this risk, if consumers are willing to pay for this service. One approach is a financial instrument with a return tied to the rate of college-cost inflation, such as the certificate of deposit (CD) offered by the College Savings Bank (see Chapter 5). Chapter 6 discusses the problems involved in offering financial instruments tied to inflation indices. It is important to note that on average over the past several years, I could have earned a higher return by investing in common stocks than in the CDs offered by the College Savings Bank. But I would have had to face the worry that the stock market might underperform its long-run average, or that tuition might increase at a faster rate than anticipated. The success of the College Savings Bank is an indication that at least some people are willing to pay (in the sense of accepting a lower expected return) for the insurance that the bank is providing.

The financial markets have been impressively innovative in recent years in developing new financial instruments designed to meet unfilled needs. The growth of futures and options markets is an important example of this innovation, and such instruments may be useful in connection with our current topic.

Futures Contracts

Consider a tuition futures contract. This contract might equal the cost of one year's Yale tuition (or an average of Yale, Ohio State, and University of Houston, for example). Each contract would be for a particular year such as 1999 or 2005, and would trade on a futures exchange. Each contract would involve an obligation to buy or sell a year's Yale tuition, with settlement on September 1 of each year. That is, no payment is made when the contract is entered into (except for a margin requirement that must be maintained). The price would be determined in the market between buyers and sellers. The Yale 2005 contract might sell today for $45,000. That is, the buyer would commit to paying $45,000 in September 2005 and at that time would receive an amount equal to whatever the Yale tuition was for 2005. If that tuition were $65,000, the buyer would have a $20,000 profit; if it were $30,000, the buyer would have a $15,000 loss.

One could use this device for gambling or speculating, but it is not necessarily a gamble. The contract would provide a potential student with a means of hedging against the risk of unexpected tuition increases. A family could set up a savings program that would accumulate $45,000 by 2005 with the assurance that it would be sufficient to meet the 2005 tuition requirement. That is, if tuition turns out to be $70,000, that is the amount that will be received from the futures contract.

It is clear that there would be potential buyers of such futures contracts. But a deal requires two parties. Who would be the sellers? In principle, the price would reflect the relative numbers of buyers and sellers. Ignore for the moment the possibility that Yale or other colleges may have an interest in selling futures contracts. Speculators might be brought into the marketplace by the opportunity to earn profits. Suppose that the best estimate of 2005 Yale tuition is $40,000. The speculator could expect to make a profit on this transaction by selling a futures contract at $45,000. The buyer may have the same expectation that $40,000 is the best estimate of 2005 tuition, but is willing to enter into the contract at $45,000 to eliminate uncertainty and to protect against the risk that tuition might actually turn out to be $60,000 or $80,000.

This is a very neat device in principle, although it probably would not work. There are many very successful futures contracts being actively traded, but some proposed futures contracts have not developed as their sponsors hoped. Speculators play a role in all these markets, but most successful markets are in those contracts in which there are parties with a logical business interest on both sides, as in the traditional agricultural commodities. A futures market is viable only if there is a significant volume of transactions, so that traders can profit. In futures markets, that requires considerable day-to-day price volatility. It is hard for me to see expectations of tuition levels years in the future changing very much over the short run. That is, if the market opens today, potential buyers and sellers will make their contracts, but there will be little reason for additional buying and selling of these contracts to take place tomorrow.

Options

More important, the tuition futures contract is not the ideal instrument to meet the needs of most parents worried about future tuition costs. The principal fear is that tuition costs may soar out of sight. What is wanted is insurance against this risk. The financial instrument most relevant to this concern is the option. A tuition futures option would give the buyer the right to claim an amount equal to Yale tuition in, say, 2005 for $40,000. If tuition turns out to be $60,000, there will be a profit on the option; if tuition is less than $40,000, the option will not be exercised. In view of the fear of rapidly rising tuition, it is reasonable to expect that many families would be willing to pay a reasonable amount for what is really insurance against excessive increases in tuition.

Finance theory allows us to calculate the fair value of such an option, and to value that option independently of individual consumers' attitudes toward risk. In combination with a savings program (or an estimate of ability to pay out of current income), an option would provide the assurance that tuition costs can be met. A savings program alone cannot usually provide this assurance without severe limits on spending in the precollege years. The prepayment plans do provide the desired insurance, but introduce the additional risk of not using the paid-for tuition if the student does not attend a covered college.

I have made some estimates of the fair value of an option as I have described it: 2005 Yale tuition ($16,300 in 1991-92) at an exercise price of $30,000 would have a cost of $5,173; at an exercise price of $40,000 (which is what tuition will be if it increases at a rate of 7 percent per year), it would have a cost of $1,618; at an exercise price of $60,000, it would have a cost of $1.58. Depending on one's attitude toward risk and estimated ability to make up a shortfall from savings, these prices may seem attractive to some people.

While it would be nice if such an instrument existed, I see little likelihood that the private sector would have the incentives to develop such a market. Perhaps this is a reasonable role for the state or federal government to play. It is a simpler and lesser role than that of providing a prepaid tuition program, yet it accomplishes all the objectives claimed for prepaid tuition plans. It would encourage saving by those with the economic resources to do so and it would eliminate the risk to the future college student that costs may soar out of sight. Of course, like the prepayment plans, it does not eliminate the risk of soaring college costs, but simply shifts that risk to the state.

I believe that the risk of rapidly rising college costs is greatly overstated. As this exercise has shown, the fair cost of protecting against this risk is not prohibitive. I don't know whether consumers would be willing to pay very much for the option I have described, but it appears that a state could provide such an option to its citizens at a modest cost and at modest risk. A survey by Robert D. Mettlen of a relevant sample of parents concerns their potential interest in something very close to the instrument I have described—an option tied not to Yale tuition, but to the very low Texas tuition rates.[4] My calculation of the value of an option on Texas tuition, with an exercise price of $1,500 annual tuition in 2005, is $944. The price of such an option with an exercise price of $4,500 would be $168. If the state of Texas were to offer such options, it would bear only one risk—that tuition would increase beyond the strike price. It would not be simultaneously facing the risk that investment returns might be less than the rate of tuition increase. Furthermore, the state has some control over the risk it is facing.

SUBSIDIZATION OF TUITION

If I am right about the limited economic attractiveness of prepaid tuition plans, why have they been so successful in attracting purchasers where they have been tried, namely, in Michigan and Florida? I believe that much of their popularity has been due to underpricing. Jeffrey Lehman, in Chapter 3 of this book, discusses the underpricing in Michigan, where contracts were offered at less than current tuition rates. The Florida underpricing is not so obvious, but it illustrates an important element of tuition risk—the subsidization of tuition by the state.

Most college tuitions are subsidized, in part, by income on endowments and by contributions. In most private colleges the extent of such subsidization is modest, but in some state systems the current subsidy is very large. Tuition and fees at the University of Houston are now $1,500, and they are only slightly higher at Florida state colleges. Today's tuition in these states is an incredible bargain. This is perhaps the only significant service in the economy that is available to the general public at a fraction of its actual production cost. But parents have a legitimate fear that this bargain may not last. There are several reasons why some states may reduce the extent to which they are subsidizing college tuition. One is economic efficiency. Low tuition, like an unduly low price on any commodity, may stimulate excessive consumption; that is, low tuition may attract students who would not otherwise be in college. However valid that may be as an economic proposition, I doubt that many states will cut tuition subsidies on the basis of that sort of reasoning. Much more likely is a decision based on the state's financial condition. A number of states are in dire financial straits, or at least think they are. And citizens of some states, such as Texas, are unwilling to tax themselves sufficiently to pay for the services they would like. It would not be surprising if some states decided to sharply increase tuition as a result.

Such reactions in the future would not be irrational, since the subsidy itself can be attacked on equity grounds. The subsidy is the same for all who pay full tuition. Much of the benefit therefore goes to the wealthy. Some analysts suggest that the current system exists precisely because of this fact. A simple alternative would be to increase tuition to cover all or much of the costs, and provide financial assistance to those who need it. It is hard to argue against such a change on either economic or equity grounds.

Such a change could be devastating to a family prepared to handle future tuition increases averaging 6 or 8 or 10 percent, but unable to cope with a sudden 200 percent increase. Such a family would rationally pay a significant amount to protect against the subsidy being reduced. In my view, this is the real attraction of state-run prepaid tuition plans—a factor that is more political than economic. Note that no private party can easily give a guarantee of financial protection against such a change in state policy. The state can do so because it controls tuition. Robert Bowman, the Michigan State Treasurer, emphasizes the state's control over tuition as essential to the financial soundness of the Michigan Education Trust program.[5] Of course, a prepaid tuition plan does limit the state's flexibility on tuition, but those who want to prevent the state from significantly reducing the subsidy favor that restriction of flexibility. I believe that this is the heart of the interest in prepaid tuition plans; they are a means of preserving the historical tuition subsidy for the wealthy in low-tuition states. I find that a weak reed on which to base a major government program.

NOTES

1. *Digest of Education Statistics*, Washington, D.C.: Department of Education, 1989.

2. "Invitational Conference on College Prepayment and Savings Plans," sponsored by the American Council on Education, the College Board, the Education Commission of the States, and the National Center for Postsecondary Governance and Finance, 1987.

3. Ibid.

4. Robert D. Mettlen, "Prepaid Tuition Plans: Markets and Institutions," IHELG Monograph No. 92-5, 1992.

5. "Invitational Conference on College Prepayment and Savings Plans," sponsored by the American Council on Education, the College Board, the Education Commission of the States, and the National Center for Postsecondary Governance and Finance, 1987.

Chapter 3

The Distribution of Benefits from Prepaid Tuition Programs: New Empirical Evidence About the Effects of Program Design on Participant Demographics

Jeffrey S. Lehman

The Michigan Education Trust (MET), was the most widely publicized government action in the field of higher education finance during the 1980s. MET allowed parents of young children to purchase contracts that would later pay for tuition at Michigan's public colleges. MET promised to protect parents against the perceived risk that college would become unaffordable by the time their children were ready to enroll. Widely heralded as a bold innovation emulated by other states, MET was considered Governor James Blanchard's preeminent legislative achievement during his two terms in office.

Today, the bloom is off the rose. Governor Blanchard is out of office, and MET is in disarray. Concerns about MET's solvency have led the MET board to suspend sales of new prepaid tuition contracts. The new state treasurer describes the program as "a deal that was too good to be true," and the once-glowing press reviews have turned sour.[1] (See Chapter 5.)

I have argued elsewhere that students of public policy can learn a great deal from the worst mistake of the MET board.[2] During its first year of operation, the board set prices for MET contracts, and it set them

Jeffrey S. Lehman is professor of law and public policy at the University of Michigan Law School.

way too low. I believe that this error resulted from the interaction between certain widely prevalent political incentives and the breakdown of the cultural institutions that ordinarily counteract them. Moreover, in the long run this error is likely to redistribute wealth upward in Michigan, assisting wealthy contract holders to the detriment of working- and middle-class taxpayers.

In this chapter, however, I shall argue that students of public policy can also learn a great deal from the most admirable action of the MET board. During its third year of operation, the board decided to change the terms on which MET participants could pay for their contracts. The board authorized the sale of contracts under a "monthly purchase/payroll deduction plan," hereafter referred to as the monthly payment option (MPO). The hope was that families who could not afford to pay the total cost of a MET contract in advance would be able to buy the contracts on the installment plan.

This change in policy provides an interesting natural experiment. Do the terms of purchase really affect the income distribution of program participants? Was the state able to induce more lower-income families to participate by (in effect) offering to lend them the purchase price? More generally, is the skewed distribution of participants in prepaid tuition programs primarily a function of credit market failure—the inability of low-income families to borrow against future earnings?

This chapter first describes the early history of MET, from Governor Blanchard's initial call for the creation of a "Baccalaureate Education Savings Trust" through the sale of approximately 39,000 contracts in the fall of 1988. It then summarizes a critique of MET that I published in the summer of 1990 and the political response to that critique—in particular, the decision in the fall of 1990 to establish the monthly payment option. Next, it examines data about the distribution of monthly payment option contracts to determine the distributional consequences of the new program. Finally, it offers some general interpretations of these findings and suggests their significance for future policymakers.

EARLY HISTORY OF MET

MET was the nation's first government-sponsored prepaid college tuition program. It sold contracts to parents (and grandparents) of young children, promising to pay the tuition (including all mandatory fees, but not room and board) of any beneficiary child who ended up attending one of Michigan's 15 public four-year colleges and universities. The contracts provided that MET would cover the state-resident tuition for any beneficiary who attended a Michigan public college. If the beneficiary did not attend a Michigan public college, he or she could obtain a prorated cash refund that roughly approximated the average in-state tuition prevailing at Michigan public colleges during the student's senior year in high school.

Governor Blanchard first proposed a state-run prepaid tuition program in his State of the State Address on January 30, 1986, and he signed the Michigan Education Trust Act before the end of that year. The Act created MET as an autonomous subunit within the Michigan Department of Treasury, managed by a nine-member board of directors. Its assets are not considered state money and may not be loaned or transferred to the state (although they may be pooled with state pension funds for investment purposes). If MET becomes insolvent, the state has no statutory obligation to bail it out; rather, whatever assets of MET remain are to be immediately prorated among the investors.[3]

During the summer of 1988, MET announced a price schedule for the first year's contracts. The cost of a MET contract, covering four years of tuition, ranged from $6,756 for a newborn baby to $9,152 for a child entering tenth grade in the fall of 1988. That fall, 38,842 contracts were purchased, at a total purchase cost of $261,493,807.[4]

In establishing prices for the first cohort, the MET board approved a somewhat controversial set of actuarial assumptions. The most significant of those assumptions concerned (1) the relationship between future tuition inflation and MET's pretax future earnings and (2) the federal income tax treatment of MET. Those assumptions enabled MET to sell contracts at prices discounted by up to 25 percent off then-prevailing tuition rates.[5]

CRITICISM OF THE PROGRAM

In my 1990 article, I made two sets of empirical assertions. First, I stated that the MET board had set prices too low in 1988, based on the information that was available to the board at that time. "[I]f MET had made more appropriate tax and actuarial assumptions, it would have collected almost 50 percent more from the program's participants than it did—over $100 million more."[6] Second, I stated that if future taxpayers are required to make up for that mistake by allowing MET contract purchasers to keep the benefit of their bargain, "the undeniable net effect will be a transfer of wealth up the income distribution."[7]

My assertion that the MET board had set prices too low followed from several corrections to the actuarial assumptions that the board had given to its actuaries. Two corrections were particularly significant. First, even though tuition inflation over the prior two decades had held fairly constant at 8.7 percent per year (approximately equal to the average annual pretax total return on a diversified portfolio over that period), MET had assumed that tuition inflation over the following 18 years would average 7.3 percent (2.5 percent less than MET's assumed pretax return).[8] Second, even though it had not sought a private letter ruling from the Internal Revenue Service (IRS) or even a formal opinion letter from its law firm, the board had based its price on a federal tax assumption that was "the most daring of the [plausible] options."[9]

My assertion that a bailout of MET would be regressive was based on two different sources of data about who had bought MET contracts. In May 1989, MET issued a news release purporting to show the percentage of MET families whose adjusted gross income fell into each of five brackets. At approximately the same time, MET also released the distribution of all MET participants by ZIP codes. I used both sources of data to compare these participants with representative reference populations of families, children, and public college freshmen. I concluded that "[n]o matter which set of figures one uses, it remains obvious that MET beneficiaries are not representative of the typical Michigan child. MET participants are far more heavily concentrated in the wealthier reaches of the population than in any of the plausible reference groups."[10]

RESPONSES TO CRITICISM

When my article appeared, then–Governor Blanchard and then–Treasurer Bowman promptly denounced it as politically motivated.[11] The controversy was (for a brief moment) front-page news.[12] For the most part, editorial writers took the charitable position that my article had, at a minimum, raised important questions about the way MET had been implemented.[13]

But mine was not the only criticism of MET to surface and receive public attention during 1990. In March, Peter Boettke of Oakland University released a paper criticizing MET.[14] In November, Paul Horvitz of the University of Houston released an analysis of MET.[15]

Change in Methods of Payment

It is not surprising that in the midst of controversy over MET the state government did not merely remain passive. In an effort to shore up MET's solvency, Governor Blanchard successfully pressured state colleges to minimize tuition increases.[16] At the same time, the MET board moved to respond to MET's country-club image. At special meetings on August 29, 1990, and September 21, 1990, the board approved the sale of monthly payment option contracts during the coming autumn's enrollment period.[17]

Table 3.1. Cost of Monthly Payment Options Contracts (for four years of tuition)

Expected Year of Matriculation	Lump-Sum Contract Cost	Monthly Cost, 4-Year MPO	Monthly Cost, 7-Year MPO	Monthly Cost, 10-Year MPO
2008	$8,380	$216	$140	$112
2007	8,540	220	144	114
2006	8,704	224	146	116
2005	8,888	228	150	118
2004	9,084	236	152	120
2003	9,296	240	156	124
2002	9,516	244	160	126
2001	9,748	252	164	130
2000	9,972	256	168	
1999	10,196	264	172	
1998	10,356	268	174	
1997	10,504	272		
1996	10,648	276		
1995	10,780	280		

The monthly payment option enabled contract purchasers to deviate from the traditional lump-sum method of purchasing contracts, spreading payments over a period of 4, 7, or 10 years as shown in Table 3.1.[18] (See Table 3.6 for the effective interest charges involved.) In addition to the amounts shown in Table 3.1, the purchaser was also required to pay an extra $25 each year after the first year of participation in the monthly payment option.

The monthly payment option was indeed popular. Partway through the 1990 enrollment period, which extended from October 15 through November 9, MET issued a press release declaring that it had appointed a "liaison for the new payroll deduction plan, due to the overwhelming response MET has received since the payment option was introduced."[19] That burst of enthusiasm may have been premature; ultimately it turned out that MET contract sales fell by 41 percent from the level of the previous year. Nonetheless, more than one-third of the new contracts were bought through the monthly payment option.[20]

As I will show in more detail later, the creation of the monthly payment option had little effect on the income distribution of MET participation. Nevertheless, the 1990 enrollment period may well prove to have been a watershed for MET, for reasons largely unrelated to the program itself. Two days before the close of the enrollment period, Michigan voters awoke to the surprising news that Democratic Governor Blanchard had been defeated by Republican John Engler.[21] Although Engler had voted for MET as a state senator in 1986, he had become a vocal critic of the program during his gubernatorial campaign.[22]

Change in State Administration

Almost immediately after the election results were final, Engler indicated that MET would be examined carefully. He said that the state would honor tuition contracts that have already been taken out but hinted that future buyers might be looking at higher prices. "I think we're $50 million to $100 million short right now."[23]

During 1991, the Engler administration adopted a decidedly more guarded attitude toward MET. In late spring, the new state treasurer publicly voiced skepticism about the program's ability to sustain itself in the future.[24] Consistent with those doubts, the newly reconfigured MET board first voted to ask the state legislature to acknowledge a moral obligation to bail the program out in the event of insolvency.[25] The board then declined to sell new MET contracts during 1991, proposing instead that the state sell college savings bonds (see Chapter 5) similar to those sold by 23 other states.[26]

Thus, the change from a Democratic to a Republican administration increased official willingness to acknowledge the possibility that MET contracts had been sold too cheaply. (It is, of course, not at all surprising that the new administration would be willing to suggest that its predecessor mishandled the implementation of a new program.) Moreover, the Engler administration renounced its predecessor's practice of attempting to enforce program solvency by restricting universities' ability to raise tuition revenues.[27]

Yet, the Engler administration is decidedly unwilling to take the public position that if MET is ultimately found to be insolvent, contract holders should receive less than the full benefit of their bargains with the Blanchard administration. Notwithstanding what is widely referred to as a state fiscal "crisis," and notwithstanding the fact that the state has no statutory obligation to bail out MET, Governor Engler has persisted in the view that if MET becomes insolvent, the taxpayers have a "moral obligation" to ensure that program beneficiaries receive more than just a refund of their purchase costs and a proportionate share of MET's earnings.[28]

A variety of factors are surely relevant to the question of whether the state has a moral obligation to give MET participants an extraordinary return on their investments—a return that was promised, but may prove unattainable without public subsidy. The unequivocal promises of former Governor Blanchard surely strengthen the case for such a moral obligation.[29] The more precise language of the MET contracts, however, might tend to weaken it, as might public warnings from commentators that the deal was "too good to be true."[30] Perhaps more important, the MET board could weaken the case for such a moral obligation still further by coming forward now, only a few years into the program, and offering all participants the opportunity to withdraw.[31]

In contemplating the appropriateness of a bailout, such considerations of equity should be supplemented by attention to distributional concerns. Who would be required to fund such a bailout? Who would benefit? How do the contract holders' particular claims of need and dessert fit into more general claims of need and dessert in a society feeling the pinch of scarcity?

As it was originally designed, MET drew its participants disproportionately from the more advantaged sectors of the state population. The current political situation gives special significance to the question of whether that distributional pattern was altered by the introduction of the monthly payment option. According to former Treasurer Bowman, that was the reason for the change.[32] Did it work?

DISTRIBUTIONAL EFFECTS OF THE MPO

The executive director of MET furnished me with the distribution by ZIP codes of the 1,864 purchasers of contracts in 1990 who selected either the monthly purchase plan or the payroll deduction plan. Of these contracts, 22 reflected purchasers from ZIP codes outside Michigan, and another 15 showed ZIP codes for which reliable data were not obtainable from the Census Bureau. That left a usable within-Michigan base of 1,827 contracts.[33]

The Michigan ZIP codes can be ranked according to median family income, enabling us to determine the extent to which participants in MET's plan are drawn from families who live in high-income areas. Table 3.2 shows the percentage of monthly payment option contracts purchased by families in each quintile of the population (ranked by the median income of their ZIP codes).[34] A comparison of this income distribution with that of other reference populations shows whether the MPO accomplished its goal of increasing MET's "accessibility." Table 3.2 certainly of-

Table 3.2. Income Distribution of MPO Contract Purchasers (1990)

Population Segment	Share of MPO Contracts (%)
Richest fifth	39
Next fifth	22
Next fifth	17
Next fifth	15
Poorest fifth	7

fers little comfort to those who would contend that the monthly payment option makes a positive contribution to the cause of distributional justice.

A proper analysis of the problem should not end, however, with a simple descriptive table. Questions concerning the distributional impact of public policy necessarily require one to pay explicit attention to the question, "Compared to what?" If monthly payment option contracts are supposed to increase access to higher education, the increase should be measured by reference to some other identifiable situation. Precisely which improvement one has in mind determines the appropriate reference group against which the distribution of contracts should be compared.

One plausible reference group consists of all children living in Michigan. I assume that families improve their financial well-being by purchasing MET contracts. If that is the case, it is useful to know how financial well-being is distributed among Michigan children generally. If financial well-being is generally more skewed than the distribution of MPO contracts, one might plausibly argue that the contracts are redistributing wealth toward the less fortunate.

Table 3.3 compares the distribution of MPO contracts with the distribution of family income among all children in Michigan (families without children are excluded). It suggests that the sale of MPO contracts has distributed financial benefits in a way that is even more skewed toward high-income taxpayers than the overall distribution of income. If (as I believe), the enjoyment of this financial benefit by MET contract holders will ulti-

Table 3.3. Comparision of Income Distribution of MPO Contract Purchasers and Overall Family Income in Michigan (1990)

Population Segment	Share of MPO Contracts (%)	Share of Family Income (%)
Richest fifth	39	28
Next fifth	22	22
Next fifth	17	20
Next fifth	15	17
Poorest fifth	7	13

mately require a subsidy from Michigan taxpayers, the sale of monthly payment option contracts appears to constitute a taxpayer-financed transfer of wealth up the income distribution.

One might argue, however, that the reference group used in Table 3.3 is inappropriate, and that the income distribution of MPO contract purchasers should be compared to that of the families who were sending their children to state universities before MET was in place. The argument might go as follows: "Public higher education is a sensible public investment, whose benefits redound to all the citizenry. MET is a program designed to make public higher education more accessible than it currently is. As long as the distribution of MPO contracts is less concentrated than the pre-MET distribution of freshmen, the program is doing its job."

Once again, however, the data appear to undermine any claim that the sale of monthly payment option contracts improves access to higher education for families who might not otherwise be able to afford it.

The best that can be said about the MPO is shown in Table 3.5, that the income distribution of its purchasers is not as badly skewed as that of the purchasers of MET contracts in 1988, when the MPO was not available. Unfortunately, all of the difference in participation by the poorest fifth may be accounted for by a difference in the way the data were reported in 1988 and in 1990.[35] Moreover, even if the data were perfectly comparable, Table 3.5 would not necessarily demonstrate that the avail-

Table 3.4. Comparison of Income Distribution of MPO Contract Purchasers (1990) and All Freshmen Attending Michigan Public Universities (1988)

Population Segment	Share of 1990 MPO Contracts (%)	Share of 1988 Freshmen (%)
Richest fifth	39	33
Next fifth	22	21
Next fifth	17	17
Next fifth	15	16
Poorest fifth	7	13

ability of the MPO improved the distribution of all 1990 MET contract
sales over that of 1988. (The distribution of non-MPO MET contracts in
1990 may have been more skewed than it was in 1988, given that the
monthly payment option was available!)

How does one determine which table is the "right" one for purposes
of policy analysis? It depends on which alternative situation provides the
proper baseline against which to evaluate the current program. The question is ultimately one of politics, not logic.[36] We must determine
whether, as a matter of public perception and political compromise, MET
is a necessary part of the political scene. If so, then marginal improvements in the distribution of its benefits are significant. But if there were a
realistic possibility that MET could be transformed in ways that offered
even greater net improvements along the relevant policy dimensions (including distributive justice), we should not accept the MPO as an adequate response to MET's shortcomings.

EVALUATION AND CONCLUSION

Why did the MPO not have a more radical effect on the income distribution of MET participants? A number of possibilities suggest themselves.

Perhaps the most obvious is that the implicit credit terms of the
monthly payment option were not sufficiently attractive. A comparison of

Table 3.5. Comparison of Income Distribution of MPO Contract
Purchasers (1990) and MET Contract Purchasers (1988)

Population Segment	Share of 1990 MPO Contracts (%)	Share of 1988 MET Contracts (%)
Richest fifth	39	50
Next fifth	22	22
Next fifth	17	13
Next fifth	15	11
Poorest fifth	7	4

the lump-sum prices and the monthly payments in Table 3.1 shows that MET was effectively charging interest at roughly 11 or 12 percent annually for the privilege of participating in the MPO. (See Table 3.6.)

But there must also be other reasons. Despite the relatively high interest rates, 1,864 families found those terms attractive. The puzzle is to determine why, among those 1,864 families, the income distribution remained so badly skewed toward the high end.

My own conjecture is that the amount of the required monthly payment matters much more than the implicit interest rate. A prospective monthly payment option contract purchaser is not merely choosing between paying $8,380 now and paying $112 per month for the next 10 years. Rather, the choice for such a purchaser is probably between paying

Table 3.6. Effective Annual Interest Rates of MPOs Assuming Monthly Compounding (1990)

Expected Year of Matriculation	4-Year MPO (%)	7-Year MPO (%)	10-Year MPO (%)
2008	11.8	11.1	11.2
2007	11.8	11.5	11.2
2006	11.7	11.3	11.1
2005	11.5	11.5	11.0
2004	12.3	11.2	10.9
2003	11.9	11.3	11.1
2002	11.5	11.3	10.9
2001	11.9	11.3	11.1
2000	11.5	11.4	
1999	12.0	11.4	
1998	12.0	11.3	
1997	12.0		
1996	12.1		
1995	12.2		

$112 per month for the next 10 years (and receiving a MET contract), and not purchasing a MET contract at all.

A MET contract is a form of dedicated savings. A low-income family is less able to divert savings from another form into a MET contract; the monthly payment is more likely to come out of current consumption. Given that higher-income people have higher marginal propensities to save, it is not surprising that they dominate all forms of MET contract purchases.

In 1989, the average pretax cash income for the lowest fifth of U.S. families with children was $662 per month; for the next-highest fifth it was $1,722 per month.[37] Those figures alone make it unsurprising that relatively few low-income families bought MET contracts, even on the monthly plan. Moreover, a MET contract may well be *less valuable* to low-income purchasers than to higher-income purchasers. For low-income families, the MET contract is more likely to displace other forms of financial aid that might otherwise have been available to their children.

For a designer of prepaid tuition programs, these findings should not be discouraging. They do not mean that prepaid tuition programs are a bad idea overall, or even from the point of view of distributional equity. Rather, these findings serve to confirm that any prepaid tuition program, however it is designed, is likely to draw primarily from the higher levels of the income distribution. That fact is disturbing when, as in Michigan, the program has been designed to subsidize program participants; it would be much less disturbing if the program had been priced so as to avoid providing such a subsidy. Indeed, if the program were charging participants a premium for this special kind of tuition insurance, we would undoubtedly be relieved to learn that most of the burden of that premium was falling on those best able to bear it.[38]

Sliding-Scale Systems

The only way to make a substantial difference in the distribution of program participants would be to adopt a sliding-scale price system, which would charge most participants equally, but would also provide subsidies to low-income contract purchasers. If one were to implement such a system directly, through the prepaid tuition program itself, one would undoubtedly create an administrative nightmare. Moreover, providing such redistributive subsidies internally, through funds raised from other purchasers, would strain the solvency of the program.

But there is another way. A program could piggyback on the tax system. The program could charge prices that did not vary with participant income. Low-income participants could then recoup part of the contract cost from the tax system by claiming a refundable credit on their tax returns for the year of the purchase; the amount of the credit would depend on the purchaser's taxable income for federal income tax purposes. (For example, if the purchase price for a newborn was $12,000, the credit could be set equal to 30 percent of the extent to which the purchaser's taxable income fell short of $30,000). Because the funds for the subsidy would come out of general revenues, they would not affect the actuarial soundness of the program.

Setting Price Structures

The moral of this story is that the price structure of a prepaid tuition program matters on several levels. It affects not only the program's solvency, but also its distributional equity. The effect on distributional equity does not arise because changes in the ways participants can finance the purchase of a contract are likely to influence who will participate. If the price structure adopted is not a sliding-scale structure, new financing options are unlikely to have much effect on participation, which will inevitably be skewed toward society's most advantaged.

Distributional considerations suggest that a prepaid tuition program should not embody a generalized, across-the-board subsidy. If a state wishes to broaden the base of participation, it should implement a sliding-scale price structure indirectly, through a system of tax credits. But whether or not it chooses to do so, the state should view skeptically any proposal to price the program in a way that (explicitly or implicitly) offers a generalized subsidy to all participants. The nominal contract price should reflect the fair market value of the contract.

NOTES

1. "Michigan Flunks Its Tuition Trust Fund," *Wall Street Journal* (March 20, 1992):C1.

2. Jeffrey S. Lehman, "Social Irresponsibility, Actuarial Assumptions, and Wealth Redistribution: Lessons About Public Policy from a Prepaid Tuition Program," *Michigan Law Review* 88 (1990):1035.

3. 1986 Mich. Pub. Acts 316, Mich. Comp. Laws Sections 390.1421 et seq.

4. Coopers & Lybrand, *Michigan Education Trust Actuary's Report on 1988 Enrollments* 1(1989):5-11 (hereafter, 1989 Actuary's Report). An additional 1,567 contracts (having a purchase cost of $3,946,084) were sold that provide for more restricted benefits than the standard contract described in the text. In March 1990, the actuaries made a "data adjustment" and concluded that 38,860 full-benefits contracts were sold. Coopers & Lybrand, *Michigan Education Trust Actuary's Report: Valuation as of September 30, 1989* (1990):9 (hereafter, 1990 Actuary's Report). In February 1991, the actuaries made more data adjustments and reduced the number to 38,858. Coopers & Lybrand, *Michigan Education Trust Actuary's Report: September 30, 1990* (February 1991):9,10 (hereafter, 1991 Actuary's Report). In January 1992, the actuaries stood their ground. Coopers & Lybrand, *Michigan Education Trust Actuary's Report: September 30, 1991* (January 1992):9 (hereafter, 1992 Actuary's Report).

5. In 1989, tuitions at Michigan public colleges rose by approximately 9 percent, and the board raised the prices of contracts by amounts ranging up to 16 percent. For a newborn, the cost went up to $7,840; for a tenth grader, the cost went up to $10,172. Purchasers of new full-benefits contracts fell to 8,950. 1991 Actuary's Report:13.

6. Lehman, "Lessons About Public Policy," 1107.

7. Ibid., 1113.

8. Ibid., 1072-1081.

9. Ibid., 1098, 1127-1132. Specifically, the board assumed that while MET would be taxed as a corporation, it would not have to include in its income the amounts it received by selling contracts, but would be able to deduct all tuition payments on behalf of a student to the extent they exceeded the student's original purchase cost.

   Early in its history, MET had sought a private letter ruling from the IRS, arguing that it should be wholly exempt from federal income taxation. The ruling that emerged was, however, unfavorable. Priv. Ltr. Rul. 88-25-027 (March 29, 1988).

10. Lehman, "Lessons About Public Policy," 1141.

11. I had begun raising questions about MET publicly in 1988. See Jeffrey Lehman and Kent Syverud, "Tuition Plan: Is it Just Pie in the Sky?" *Detroit Free Press*, June 8, 1988. During the summer of 1989, an assistant to John Engler, the Republican Senate Majority Leader, called to ask if I would permit Senator Engler to nominate me to serve on the MET board. (By statute, the governor appoints the board, but one seat is to be filled with an appointee nominated by the Senate Majority Leader.) I agreed to let him do so. Governor Blanchard did not act on the nomination until after my article appeared during the summer of 1990, at which time he rejected the nomination.

    While I have no doubt that Senator Engler's motivation in nominating me was a political desire to embarrass Governor Blanchard, my own motivations for studying MET have always been more prosaic.

12. See, for example, "Professor: MET Based on Bad Math," *Detroit News* (July 3, 1990):1; "MET Needs To Get Lucky—Prof," *Jackson Citizen Patriot* (July 3,

1990):*1*. See also "State Tuition Plan Shaky, U-M Professor Says in Study," *Detroit Free Press* (July 2, 1990):B3; "Trust Plan Merits a Close Look," *Crain's Detroit Business* (July 9, 1990):8; "$100 Million Shortfall in MET's Future?" *Oakland Press* (July 3, 1990):A-3; "Will the IRS Kill Tuition Trusts?" *U.S. News & World Report* (July 30, 1990):43.

13. See, for example, "More MET Threats?" *Detroit News* (July 23, 1990):6A; "Blanchard's Tuition Protests Shortchange Universities," *Detroit Free Press* (July 27, 1990):8A.

14. Peter Boettke, "The Michigan Education Trust: A Political Economy Perspective," *The Mackinac Center* (March 12, 1990).

15. Paul Horvitz, "Is MET Insolvent? An Analysis of the Financial Performance of the Michigan Education Trust Under Bank Regulatory Accounting Principles," *The College Savings Bank Research Division* (November 20, 1990).

16. See, for example, "Tuition Increase Inspires Threat from Governor," *New York Times* (August 5, 1990):36; "Tuition Ultimatum: Blanchard Will Cut Funding if Colleges Exceed Guidelines," *Ann Arbor News* (July 25, 1990):A1. In response to that pressure, the universities ultimately settled on tuition increases for 1990 averaging only 6.5 percent.

17. Michigan Education Trust Board of Directors Meeting Minutes, August 29, 1990; September 21, 1990. The increase in the price of contracts ranged up to 7 percent above the previous year's prices. For a newborn, the cost went up to $8,380; for a tenth grader, the cost went up to $10,908.

18. The monthly payment option took two forms. Under the monthly purchase plan, the purchaser makes direct payments to MET each month, over a period of 4, 7, or 10 years. The payroll deduction plan requires the same level of monthly payment, but a participating employer withholds payments directly from the purchaser's paycheck.

19. PR Newswire, October 23, 1990 (available on NEXIS).

20. In 1990, a total of 5,202 contracts were purchased: 4,959 providing benefits at four-year colleges, and 243 providing benefits only at community colleges. Of that total, 1,864 were bought through the monthly payment option. 1992 Actuary's Report, 15-19.

21. Engler had been trailing in the polls by as much as 26 percent only a month before election day. See "Engler Feels He Won First Debate," UPI wire service (October 7, 1990) (available on NEXIS).

22. See, for example, "Engler Accuses Blanchard Administration of MET Fraud," UPI wire service, March 15, 1990 (available on NEXIS). See also the author's comments in note 11.

23. "Engler Says Careful Assessment, Paring Back, Will Be Done," UPI wire service, November 9, 1990 (available on NEXIS).

24. "Prepaid Tuition Plan Faces Price Hike," *Detroit News* (May 10, 1991):1A. UPI wire service, June 7, 1991 (available on NEXIS).

25. "Tuition Plan Wants Firm Backing," *Ann Arbor News* (August 7, 1991):A1.

26. "State May Scrap MET Tuition Plan," *Detroit News* (December 3, 1991):1A. PR Newswire, December 4, 1991 (available on NEXIS); "State to Offer Alternative to MET," *Detroit News* (December 5, 1991):2B.

27. See "Bill Would Tie Tuition Increases to Inflation," *Ann Arbor News* (August 1, 1991):C1. (quoting Engler spokesman saying that "the governor continues to respect the autonomous nature of the universities").

28. "Tuition Plan Wants Firm Backing," *Ann Arbor News* (August 7, 1991):A1. ("[Engler spokesman] Truscott said Blanchard and Bowman oversold the program. 'It was sold to the people with the understanding that it was guaranteed by the state,' he said. 'It clearly is not, so Governor Engler is trying to take steps now to make sure it will be guaranteed.' We still believe the people weren't told the truth about the program,' said Engler Press Secretary John Truscott. 'We're doing our best to cover the people who have purchased the contracts.'")

29. See the statements quoted in Lehman, "Lessons About Public Policy," 1120-1121.

30. Lehman and Syverud, "Pie in the Sky?"

31. See Jeffrey S. Lehman, "MET Needs a Different Kind of Bailout," *Detroit News* (August 18, 1991):3B.

32. "MET Board Sets Prices for 1990; Adopts Monthly Purchase Plan," PR Newswire, August 29, 1990 (available on NEXIS) ("'The monthly purchase plan increases the accessibility of MET for even more Michigan families,' Bowman added.").

33. The 1,864 contracts include 85 contracts associated with MET's community college program. 1992 Actuary's Report, 18-19. Those contracts account for approximately 4.5 percent of all MPO contracts. Since community college option contracts are more likely than full-benefit contracts to have been purchased by lower-income families, the data are likely to overstate any difference in distributional effect caused by the MPO.

34. See generally Lehman, "Lessons About Public Policy," 1138-1141.

35. The 1988 data do not include purchasers of contracts whose benefits were limited to community colleges; the 1990 data do include purchasers of such contracts. See the author's comments in note 33.

36. See Jeffrey S. Lehman, "To Conceptualize, To Criticize, To Defend, To Improve: Understanding America's Welfare State," *Yale Law Journal* 101(1991):685, 722-723.

37. Calculated from Committee on Ways and Means of the U.S. House of Representatives, 102nd Cong., 1st Sess., *Overview of Entitlement Programs—1991 Green Book* (Ways and Means Comm. Print 102-9):1024.

38. For a more extended discussion of the distributional issues, see Lehman, "Lessons About Public Policy," 1053-1055.

Chapter 4

State Prepaid Tuition Plans: Designing a Successful Program

William Montjoy

Prepaid tuition plans are programs designed to empower the middle class by providing economic access to higher education. For most middle-income families, current income and ordinary savings are no longer adequate to pay for a college education. Savings specifically set aside for the purpose of college education must be available when needed to pay for these expenses.[1] The middle class of America has seen itself squeezed out of numerous aid programs during the 1980s, and taxpayers are faced with a $3 billion bill each year due to rising defaults on guaranteed student loans.[2] Universities find themselves in a period of crisis, facing huge budget cuts that require administrators to do "less with less" if they are to survive.[3] One answer to these problems is to provide economic accessibility for a large segment of the population, thus ensuring future enrollments and funding streams for state colleges and universities.

National patterns in college saving clearly indicate that there is a need for government to provide an incentive to save.[4] Prepaid tuition programs increase the savings rate and help families engage in timely financial planning. For example, nearly two-thirds of the participants in the Florida Prepaid College Program contract, revealed that prior to purchasing the plan they had no specific savings for college. However, after buying a

William W. Montjoy is executive director of the Florida Prepaid Postsecondary Education Expense Board.

Florida Prepaid College Program contract, over 43 percent indicated that they had additional savings plans for other college expenses—an indication that prepaid college tuition plans have a multiplier effect that will increase the overall savings rate.[5] A state prepaid tuition program provides government service with no new taxes and at no operational cost to the state. It can be administered on the basis of a public/private partnership, creating many jobs in the private economy.[6]

For a family interested in helping its children attend college, a prepaid tuition program provides an affordable means of paying tuition over an extended period of time, with fixed monthly payments.[7] States can encourage employer/employee contribution plans and payroll deduction plans to make the financing of a prepaid tuition contract even easier.[8]

The Florida Prepaid College Program is specifically designed to implement Florida's comprehensive plan. The state's goal is to create an educational environment that allows students to develop their full potential; prevents dropouts, both in secondary school and in higher education; and encourages Florida's talented students to attend Florida colleges.[9] The Florida Prepaid College Program assists the state in reaching all these goals. For example, demographic data on college preferences are collected when prepaid contract purchasers apply to the program. These data assist in the recruitment of students for future enrollment in state colleges and universities.

Of course, all state legislatures respond to the popular demand of their constituents. The resounding success of the Florida Prepaid College Program, with over 175,000 prepaid contracts sold in just four years, is a testament to the perceived need for a prepaid tuition plan. Also, purchasers of such contracts are more likely than other residents to take an interest in their state government and to vote.

SECRETS OF SUCCESS

The primary requirement for success of a prepaid tuition plan is charging current tuition prices, without a discount. The Florida program has been widely recognized as financially sound because of this concept.[10] The program has maintained its actuarial soundness through the use of conservative assumptions.[11] It is critical to the creditability of a prepaid tuition program to have reasonable assumptions that can be verified by independent analysis.[12]

It may even be possible to have a successful program and charge a premium for a prepaid tuition contract. A purchaser of a prepaid tuition contract for a prospective student who is now only five years old may not object to paying 5 percent more than today's tuition price. Surveys have shown that the primary motivation for the purchase of a prepaid tuition contract is the guarantee that the tuition will be paid, no matter what the cost at the time of college enrollment.[13] Operational costs should be covered by a fee structure that reduces the program's need to earn a high rate of return on its investments; however, such fees should not be so high that they price a large segment of the population out of the marketplace.

In marketing a prepaid program, every effort should be made to keep it simple. One of the primary elements of success is providing a plan that the public can easily understand and use. Facilitating applications, without imposing numerous rules and guidelines, is critical to contract sales volume. Florida has averaged over 40,000 prepaid contracts each year because it has approached consumers rather than expecting them to seek out the program. Florida Prepaid College Program brochures are distributed to such locations as public and private schools, maternity wards, and state employee personnel offices. The brochure clearly discloses all contract prices in an easy-to-read fashion. Payments are made simple by the use of methods such as coupon books.

Another aspect of a successful prepaid tuition plan is the opportunity for voluntary termination. The contract should be revocable at will by purchasers, who should receive refunds of at least their principal payments. Prepaid tuition plans should not discourage participation by requiring long-term investments without any possibility of early withdrawal. A prepaid tuition contract is intended to provide peace of mind, which should not be endangered by the imposition of rigid requirements.

The Florida Prepaid College Program has quite successfully incorporated the private sector (such as banks and insurance companies) into its operations.[14] The first step in successfully convincing the private sector that a prepaid tuition plan is not a threat to the marketing of its products is to emphasize the noncompetitive aspects of the prepaid contract. For example, advertising should stress the guarantee of payment of future tuition, rather than any perceived rate of return on the premiums paid. Also, the refund of principal only, not interest, when a contract is terminated clearly demonstrates that the prepaid tuition plan is not a state-run savings account.[15] Finally, private contracting for administrative aspects of the program (for example, printing, collecting, and other administrative functions), gives private companies the opportunity to share in the revenues generated by the program.

It is critical to the continued success of a prepaid tuition plan to maintain the credibility and public confidence of present and future purchasers. Avoiding public criticism, due to unreasonable actuarial assumptions or projected investment rates of return, is the first step in this process. The Florida Legislature guarantees the financial soundness of the prepaid program.[16] Any risk to the state for future liability can be limited through a variety of statutory provisions. The enabling legislation in Florida provides that the state can terminate the program; if it does so, contracts within five years of college enrollment will be honored, and the remaining contracts will be refunded with an interest rate equal to the prevailing passbook savings rate. Investment managers handling the prepaid program portfolio must fund any shortfall that results from an imprudent investment. The program must provide annual actuarial analyses; it is also subject to the annual audit of the State Auditor General.[17]

The Florida Prepaid College Program is advertised by purchasing time on television and radio programs aimed at certain target markets. Research done prior to instituting the advertising campaign ensures that the marketing budget is effectively spent. An enrollment deadline ensures prompt purchases, thus helping to generate high sales volumes.

A program must be operated by a diversified board with nonpartisan leadership. If the public's impression is that the program has become politicized, confidence will be lost and sales will plummet. The lessons of the Michigan Education Trust (MET) in this regard should be taken to heart. To be successful, a prepaid tuition program must have three factors: conservative pricing, easy public access, and maintenance of public confidence. These three requirements can be modified to fit the particular political environment of any state to create a successful prepaid tuition plan.

RESPONSES TO CRITICISM BASED ON THE MET PLAN

In Chapter 3, Jeffrey Lehman discusses prepaid programs, based on his study of MET. Lehman's basic premise is that a prepaid tuition program will redistribute wealth up the income ladder to upper-middle-class and high-income households. This therefore creates beneficiaries of prepaid

Table 4.1. Relationship of Family Income to Type of Prepaid Tuition Contract Payment

Income	Lump Sum (%)	Installment (%)
<$20,000	5	6
$20–29,000	10	14
$30–39,000	15	19
$40–49,000	15	20
>$50,000	55	41

contracts who are not representative of typical families. The Florida data, as shown in Table 4.1, do not support this premise. Nearly 60 percent of the Florida participants have family incomes of less than $50,000. Prepaid programs are directed at middle-income households. Besides, shouldn't government incentives encourage all families to save for college, no matter what their income levels?

Another argument against Lehman's assertion of a redistribution of wealth is the absence of state subsidies in both Florida and Michigan. Lehman bases his argument on what he believes to be a virtual certainty that the Michigan program will eventually require a state subsidy to maintain its solvency. The Michigan program is, however, currently actuarially sound, based upon two independent reports by Coopers & Lybrand and Deloitte & Touche. Provided the program continues to meet its earnings assumptions, there need be no state subsidy. As described earlier, the Florida legislature has created an escape clause that allows termination in the event the program is deemed financially infeasible, with a refund at the passbook savings rate. Certainly any competent investment manager will be able to outperform passbook savings rates to create a surplus in the event of this contingency.

Whether or not a prepaid program's beneficiaries are typical of families in that state misses the point. Such programs should not be designed to reach a hypothetical median-income-level family with 2.6 children. Instead, they should provide an incentive for all families to engage in timely financial planning and should replace misguided public policies that have increased reliance on debt as a method of financing a college education.

Lehman asserts that a prepaid program will pressure state universities to minimize tuition increases to maintain the program's solvency. This is not the purpose or intent of a prepaid program. In Florida there is no link between prepaid tuition plans and tuition rates; the Florida Prepaid College Program has no relation to the level of tuition charged by the state of Florida. This fact contradicts the premise of most opposition to prepaid tuition programs—the cliche that a prepaid tuition program will be the "tail wagging the dog" regarding public universities and tuition policy.

The linkage theory breaks down once solvency is eliminated as an issue. There is obviously no need to limit tuition increases if the prepaid trust fund will remain actuarially sound. Solvency does not become an issue if contract prices are reasonably established at current tuition rates, and investment assumptions are set at conservative levels. Once the underpinnings of this premise are knocked away, most of the other arguments against prepaid tuition programs become less compelling.

Lehman claims that adding a monthly payment option to a prepaid tuition plan does not significantly change the characterization of the income distribution of the participants. Although this is difficult to define with precision, the data on the Florida program show that a slightly higher percentage of low-income families who participate do so by installments rather than by lump sums. As Table 4.1 shows, this is true at every level of lower income, and in each income category a larger percentage of persons chose installments over the lump sum option.

Lehman also asserts that permitting voluntary terminations from a prepaid plan would weaken the state's "moral obligation" to the program. If a state guarantees the prepaid tuition plan under its full faith and credit, there is no dilemma regarding a moral obligation. In Florida, where voluntary terminations are permitted, the cancellation rate is only about 10 percent. This is not high enough to disturb the actuarial calculations and can be reasonably anticipated in the program's assumptions. Politically, a provision for voluntary termination will actually strengthen a state's obligation, because the purchasers who remain are those who really want to save for their children's future college expenses.

Lehman makes an issue of the high interest rate (11 to 12 percent) on MET's installment payments. To be actuarially sound, the installment interest rate should reflect the earnings assumption. This is why the implied rate on the Florida installment option and the assumed earnings rate are both 7.5 percent. The program need only recoup its cost of lending, not make a profit on the installment plan. It may well be that had MET established a lower interest rate, the criticism would have been the reverse—the rate was not high enough.

Lehman states that the level of monthly payments matters more to most participants than the interest rate, and I agree with him. A family decision will be based on affordability before anything else. If the tuition for four years is too high for most families, consideration should be given to selling plans that cover a single years' tuition and emphasizing that plan instead of the four-year option.

Lehman's solution for the various problems he perceives for prepaid tuition plans is a complicated sliding-scale tax credit approach. As stated above, his premise for this approach is that any prepaid tuition plan is likely to draw from the upper-income portions of the population. I believe that this premise is incorrect, and that therefore the solution is false. Moreover, this kind of suggestion represents "business as usual," rather than creating an innovative approach to the problem of insufficient savings for college expenses. It is too complicated and too difficult for the buying public to understand. Such an approach would be likely to skew a program even further to the more educated, upper-income levels than MET did.

TAX IMPLICATIONS

In Chapter 5, David Williams discusses the tax implications of prepaid tuition plans, stating they have a gift tax consequence. Although this is certainly true of the MET contract, it would not appear to apply to the Florida program, because the Florida Prepaid College Program contract is revocable by the participant at will. Upon voluntary termination, only the purchaser's principal, not interest or earnings, is refunded. In fact, a $50 cancellation fee is charged for the termination, so the purchaser actually has a small loss. Clearly no ownership has been transferred, and therefore no gift has been made.

The Internal Revenue Service discussed the gift tax consequences more completely in a private letter ruling issued to the state of Indiana in 1989.[18] An authority in this field has analyzed the gift tax treatment of a purchaser of a prepaid tuition plan.[19] There are several arguments to support the position that a mere purchase is not a gift: there is no transfer of ownership or constructive ownership to the beneficiary; the contract is revocable; and the beneficiary's rights to vesting are contingent upon numerous and speculative factors. However, as stated by Williams, the gift tax treatment is not relevant for most prepaid contract purchasers, since the unified gift tax credit shields them from owing any gift tax.

It is clear that the difference between the price paid for the contract and the value of the benefit will be taxable to the beneficiary when it is received. The amount paid for the plan will be prorated on a per-credit-hour basis to determine the basis for calculating taxable income. In 1992, the Florida Prepaid College Program sent out over 2,500 Form 1099s covering usage of prepaid college contracts during the 1991 calendar year.

The most significant issue is the application of the doctrine of intergovernmental immunity to the taxation of the investment buildup of the trust fund. In Chapter 5, Williams examines in detail the arguments put forth by the federal government and MET. In a request for a private letter ruling filed in April 1990, the Florida Prepaid College Program relied on the doctrine of intergovernmental immunity, rather than performance of an essential state function under section 115 of the Internal Revenue Code; as of December 1992, no response had been received to this request.

Section 240.551(5), Florida Statutes (1991), creates the Florida Prepaid College Program as a "state agency." Section 240.551(4) creates the Prepaid College Trust Fund as a fund within the state treasury. The program's contract (Section 5.08) clearly puts purchasers on notice as to the state's intent regarding the characterization of this program:

> The state considers this an essential governmental operation to assist its citizens to access higher education. All legal and beneficial interests and the assets held in the trust fund are vested in the state for its exclusive benefit and the exclusive benefit of the colleges and universities; therefore, payments are guaranteed to be made on the beneficiary's behalf to the state college or university. Exercise of full benefits under the contract guarantees the beneficiary receipt of services and the beneficiary will not receive any funds.

Moreover, in Section 5.01 it is stated that the contract is "not a debt instrument." And finally, Section 240.551(9), Florida Statutes (1991), requires the state to meet obligations of prepaid purchasers in the event there is a shortfall.[20]

BENEFITS OF PREPAID TUITION PROGRAMS

Prepaid tuition programs provide governmental approaches to the societal problem of increasing economic access to higher education. If families have inadequate savings to finance college, and the debt they would thus incur is prohibitive, our nation will fall behind in the future "cold war," which will involve technology, not arms. Tax solutions represent "business as usual," and are too complicated for the average purchaser. Governmental programs should address the public's needs and wants without an additional tax burden; this is accomplished through plans such as the Florida Prepaid College Program.

College administrators, rather than perceiving prepaid programs as a threat to the academic community because these programs are not controlled by the education institutions, should view prepaid purchasers as a built-in constituency, ready to lobby the political leadership on behalf of higher education. Public institutions have a mission to educate the states' citizens through an open-access policy to higher education; institutional opposition to prepaid programs represents a lack of commitment to that mission. Public institutions should be quality institutions, but their admission standards should not be so unreasonably high that they prevent a state from having a future educated work force.

With proper safeguards, a taxpayer bailout or subsidy for prepaid tuition plans is not likely to be needed; the risk is minimal, and the payback is great. Can we afford not to help students save for college? Can we afford not to reduce burdensome debt and high default rates for guaranteed loans? Are we going to continue to accept increasing need for financial aid and less economic access to higher education? In the final analysis, no matter what the income distribution, payment method, or tax consequences, prepaid tuition programs represent good governmental policy.

NOTES

1. Sandy Baum, "The Need for College Savings," in Janet S. Hansen, ed., *College Savings Plans: Public Policy Choices* (New York: College Entrance Examination Board, 1990), 16.

2. Kerry Hannon, "How You're Getting Stiffed by the Student Loan Mess," *Money* (May 1992):164.

3. John Elson, "Campus of the Future," *Time* (April 13, 1992):54.

4. A. Charlene Sullivan, "Saving for College: The Investment Challenge," in *College Savings Plans*, 21.

5. State of Florida, Office of the Auditor General, *Performance Audit of the Florida Prepaid Postsecondary Education Expense Program*, Report No. 11825 (March 25, 1992):53 – 54 (hereafter, Florida Auditor General's Report No. 11825).

6. *Florida Prepaid College Program* (1992) (Annual Report) (hereafter, 1992 Annual Report).

7. *Florida Prepaid College Program* (1991) (brochure).

8. Section 240.551(1), Florida Statutes (1991).

9. Section 187.201, Florida Statutes (1991).

10. "Michigan Flunks Its Tuition Trust Fund," *Wall Street Journal* (March 20, 1992).

11. See *1992 Annual Report*. The Florida Prepaid College Trust Fund had an actuarial surplus of $26 million, based on assets of $206 million, as of June 30, 1991 (before the 1991-92 sales program).

12. State of Florida, Office of the Auditor General, *Performance Audit of the Florida Prepaid Postsecondary Education Expense Program*, Report No. 11803 (February 5, 1992):22 – 25 (hereafter, Florida Auditor General's Report No. 11803). The report's Executive Summary states unequivocally, "The Prepaid Postsecondary Education Expense Trust Fund is Actuarially Sound."

13. See Florida Auditor General's Report No. 11825:35.

14. See Florida Auditor General's Report No. 11825.

15. Sections 240.551(6)(e)1, Florida Statutes (1991).

16. Section 240.551, Florida Statutes (1991).

17. Section 240. 551(5), Florida Statutes (1991).

18. Priv. Ltr. Rul. 89-01-027 (January 6, 1989).

19. J. Timothy Philipps, "Federal Taxation of Prepaid College Tuition Plans," *Washington and Lee Law Review* 47 (1990):291, 300.

20. See J. Timothy Philipps and Edward R. Haden, "It's Not Long, But It's Not Bad: A Response to Critics of Prepaid College Tuition Plans," *University of Richmond Law Review* 26 (1992):281, 299 n.8. This article uses Florida as an example of how a program can easily be structured as an integral part of state government.

Chapter 5

Taxation of Prepaid Tuition Plans and Other Forms of College Expense Assistance

David Williams II

In 1989, I wrote an article that outlined the tax consequences of the efforts being made by both the federal government and various state governments to help defray the costs of college. Since that time, much has happened, but little has changed.[1] In the article, I concluded that preparation for future college attendance has three aspects. First, the student must study hard. Second, the family must explore many variables—such as curriculum, faculty, location, social life, reputation, and cost—to determine which institution is the best choice. Third, the financing of the college education is a vital consideration. In fact, due to the rising cost of college, this consideration must be addressed by many parents well before the other two concerns.[2] To assist parents in planning for the financing of a college education, many states have enacted some form of college expense assistance. The federal government has attempted several approaches to assist parents and students, and this paper reviews the most recent; although none were enacted, each contained items likely to resurface or be adopted by the Clinton administration and Congress. Therefore, each is examined with an eye toward the consequences of its being reconsidered. The private sector, by way of banks, insurance companies, brokerage houses, and employers, has also devised methods to help meet these rising costs.

The programs have two things in common. First, they involve some

---

David Williams II is professor of law at Ohio State University's College of Law.

sort of advance planning, purchase, or payment. For most families, the days of paying college expenses out of current earnings while a student is actually going to college are over. In addition, just putting the money in a bank and watching it slowly grow will not provide enough return. Table 5.1 demonstrates the amount one would have to put aside monthly to reach the needed goal for college costs. It assumes a 7 percent annual increase in college costs and an 8 percent return (after taxes). (It should be noted that as this book went to press in 1993, returns on most investments fell far short of this level.)

Second, the programs involve some form of tax analysis, which is essential for acquiring an understanding of the cost and benefit of each program. This chapter examines the tax implications of various forms of college-expense assistance.

FEDERAL PROGRAMS

With the exception of a very limited savings bond program, the federal government has done little to assist families in financing college. In fact, by including part of a student's scholarship in gross income[3] and denying a tax deduction for interest on student loans,[4] it has actually acted against the interests of students who require financial assistance. However, some federal initiatives described below may prove beneficial.

Table 5.1. Savings Needed to Provide for Future College Costs

| | Monthly Amount Needed | |
Years to College	Public (in-state)	Private
1	$2,881	$6,065
5	640	$1,347
8	430	906
11	335	705
15	267	563
18	236	497

Source: "How to Save for College," *Newsweek*, October 21, 1991.

U.S. Savings Bond Program

Section 135 of the Internal Revenue Code (Code of 1986), entitled "Income from United States Savings Bonds Used to Pay Higher Education Tuition and Fees," provides a limited amount of financial relief to taxpayers for their children's college educations. Section 135 allows a purchaser of qualified U.S. Savings Bonds to avoid taxation when redeeming the bonds, if the proceeds are used to pay qualified higher education expenses.[5] See definitions of "qualified U.S. Savings Bonds" and "qualified higher education expenses" below. For example, a $100 savings bond, which was purchased for $50, can be redeemed and used to pay education expenses of $100, without incurring income tax on the $50 gain. In other words, the gain is tax-free if used for education purposes. If the taxpayer uses $90 of the $100 received on redemption of the bond toward education expenses, only $40 of the $50 gain is tax-free; the remaining $10 is taxable.[6]

On the surface, this savings bond approach, whereby investments grow tax-free, seems helpful in the financing of college education.[7] However, upon closer review, the savings bond program has certain limitations that make it less valuable. First, the only bonds eligible for this special treatment are qualified U.S. Savings Bonds—those that were issued after December 31, 1989.[8] Therefore, any savings bond purchased before that date is excluded from the benefits of Section 135. Second, the only eligible expenses are those that are qualified higher education expenses, which are defined as "tuition and fees required for enrollment or attendance of the taxpayer (purchaser of the bonds), the taxpayer's spouse, or any dependent of the taxpayer" at a qualified institution.[9] This requirement actually has two drawbacks. First, while tuition and other fees are qualified expenses, payments for room and board are not. Second, if the purchaser of the bonds is the grandparent of the student, the provision does not apply unless the student is a dependent of the grandparent.

While the above reasons are enough to call into question the wisdom of Code Section 135, the real problem is the income limitation of the provision. The tax-free gain on redemption applies only if, at the time of redemption, the taxpayer meets certain adjusted gross income (AGI) requirements. The interest income exclusion is phased out for taxpayers with AGI above certain levels. For taxpayers filing joint returns, the phase-out range is from $60,000 to $90,000; for those filing single or head-of-household returns, the phase-out range is $40,000 to $50,000. If the taxpayer's AGI exceeds $60,000 ($40,000 if single or head of household), the amount of the interest that can be excluded is reduced by an amount that bears the same ratio to the amount otherwise excluded as the excess AGI bears to $30,000 ($15,000 if single or head of household).[10]

For example, Mr. and Mrs. Smith, who file a joint return, redeem a $10,000 qualified U.S. Savings Bond to pay qualified higher education expenses for their son, Robert. The $10,000 the Smiths receive represents $5,000 of principal and $5,000 of interest income. Since the qualified higher education expenses for the year were $10,000, the entire $5,000 of interest income appears to be excluded from the Smiths' gross income. However, if their AGI exceeds $60,000, there must be a phase-out reduction. If their AGI is $80,000, the phase-out reduction is $3,333, and the amount that may be excluded is $1,667, instead of $5,000. The Smiths' phase-out reduction is determined by taking the otherwise excluded amount ($5,000) and reducing it by an amount that bears the same ratio to $5,000 as the $20,000 excess AGI ($80,000 modified AGI minus $60,000 modified AGI limit) bears to $30,000 ($20,000 ÷ $30,000 or 2/3). If the Smiths' AGI is $60,000, they have zero excess AGI and are entitled to the full $5,000 exclusion. If their AGI is $90,000 or more, the phase-out reduction is $5,000, and their exclusion amount is zero.

The benefits of Code Section 135 decrease as income increases. Therefore, the federal government is saying that only individuals below a certain income level are entitled to federal assistance, in the form of favorable tax treatment, in planning for future college costs. In addition, the decision to purchase U.S. Savings Bonds today, when family income may be low or moderate, in order to fund college costs for a child 15 years later, requires a projection of the taxpayer's future AGI. In many cases, projecting AGI is quite difficult, if not impossible. The income limitation and the need to project future AGI make Section 135 of limited value to many of the people who are searching for assistance.

Senate Bill 612

During the summer of 1991, Senators Bentsen and Roth introduced Senate Bill 612 (S. 612), commonly referred to as the Bentsen-Roth IRA. While this bill was designed to assist taxpayers in a number of other areas, the financing of future college costs was one of its primary goals. S. 612 permitted individuals to create special IRA accounts designated for education. Each year an individual could contribute up to $2,000 in such a special IRA. No tax deduction would be allowed for the contribution, but the interest would be compounded tax-free (as in the case of the savings bonds, but, it was hoped, at a higher rate of return), and withdrawal from the IRA would be tax-free if used to pay qualified higher education expenses.[11]

While S. 612 sounds a lot like the savings bond program, it included two major improvements. First, the tax-free status of the earnings was not restricted or phased out according to the taxpayer's income at withdrawal; the benefits of this bill would therefore be available to many more people. Second, unlike the savings bond program, S. 612 also allowed grandparents or others to directly assist in providing tax-free financial help. In addition, this special IRA had an outstanding flexible feature. If the funds were not needed for the undergraduate education of their children, taxpayers could wait and use the funds (tax-free) for the graduate education of their children, the education of their grandchildren, the purchase of a first home for their children, or their own medical expenses as they grew older.[12]

Although S. 612 was certainly an improvement over prior governmental action, it would have been even more beneficial if (1) the contribution had been made deductible, thereby allowing before-tax dollars to be used to fund the IRA; and (2) the definition of qualified higher education expenses had been extended to include room and board costs.

Senate Bill 2159

On January 24, 1992, Senator Boren reintroduced Senate Bill 2159 (S. 2159), entitled the "Tax Fairness and Competitiveness Act of 1992." Although S. 2159 covered a number of topics, Subtitle A of the bill, "Educational Incentives," provided several measures to assist the funding of college expenses.[13]

First, the bill restored a tax deduction for interest paid on educational loans or expenses.[14] The taxpayer would have the option of either deducting the interest or taking a credit (15 percent of the interest paid, with a maximum credit of $300) against tax owed. The credit election is very important for taxpayers who do not itemize deductions and would otherwise be unable to deduct the interest paid. For example, a taxpayer whose only tax deduction was $500 of interest paid on a student loan would not itemize deductions, because the standard deduction would exceed $500. However, this provision would allow a tax credit of $75 instead of the deduction.

Second, S. 2159 expanded the definition of qualified higher education expenses to include reasonable living expenses while away from home. This appears to be the first government recognition of the fact that college costs include living expenses as well as tuition and fees. This new definition would become part of Code Section 117, thereby changing all definitions of qualified higher education expenses that refer to Section 117 (e.g., Section 135).[15]

Finally, S. 2159 expanded Section 135's exemption from gross income to include not only income from qualified U.S. Savings Bonds, but also income from any "qualified college savings account," defined as any prepaid tuition contract (state program), or any trust created or organized for the exclusive benefit of an eligible holder or his or her beneficiaries (educational trust).[16]

On its face, S. 2159 appeared to be right on target. In fact, the restoration of the interest deduction, the option of a tax credit, and the expanded definition of qualified education expenses were all excellent provisions. However, the bill had three major flaws. First, it was extremely complex and full of exceptions and limitations; therefore, any tax savings might be erased by fees paid to a tax attorney for help in understanding the bill. Second, the provision that related to the college savings accounts had an income restriction similar to the one in the savings bond program under Section 135, thus limiting access to only a portion of the population. Third, unlike the savings bond program, the college savings account provision did not provide for tax-free accumulation of earnings during the life of the investment. Therefore, unless some other provision applies, the earnings from prepaid tuition contracts and education trusts would be taxed yearly. This provision of S. 2159 was less beneficial than the existing savings bond program or the special IRA proposed by S. 612.

H.R. 4120

In his 1992 State of the Union address, former President Bush proposed certain tax measures and asked Congress to enact them by March 20, 1992. Congress passed its own tax bill, the Family Tax Fairness and Economic Growth Act of 1992, on that date, but the president did not sign it. Some of the president's proposals and some provisions of the bill passed by Congress had implications in the education finance arena.

Both then President Bush and Congress proposed allowing penalty-free (not tax-free) withdrawal of funds from an individual's IRA to pay qualified education expenses, but neither included living expenses in the definition of qualified education expenses. The Senate version of the bill, which was an outgrowth of S. 612, included penalty-free withdrawals from 401(k) and 403(b) plans as well as from IRAs. Penalty-free withdrawal was good, but tax-free withdrawal would have been better.

Although President Bush's proposals and the House version (H.R. 4120) had no provision for the expansion of the Code Section 135 savings bond program, the Senate suggested two major improvements, which were also outgrowths of S. 612. First, qualified education expenses would include those paid for any individual, not just dependents. This would allow grandparents or other persons to purchase savings bonds to help pay a student's education costs. Second, the AGI phase-out would be repealed, thus making the benefits of the program available to taxpayers in all income brackets. Both of these proposals would have been major improvements, but only the former was included in the final bill.

In the area of the taxability of student loan interest, President Bush, the House, and the Senate all had different proposals. The president suggested that interest on postsecondary education loans be allowed as an itemized deduction. The House proposed a nonrefundable tax credit for 15 percent of education loan interest with a maximum credit of $300. (In certain cases this could be increased to $500.) This credit would be phased out if the individual's AGI reached $100,000 on a joint return. The Senate version adopted the provision in S. 2159, which gave the taxpayer the option of the deduction or the credit. The final version of the bill incorporated the House proposal.

The Senate's suggestion of the creation of a "self-reliance loan" to cover higher education expenses was not included in this bill. This provision would have permitted the federal government to make loans of up to $5,000 per year for undergraduates ($15,000 for graduate students), with a lifetime cap of $30,000. The key to this provision was that repayment of the loans would be made through an addition to the student's future annual income tax liability, by using a formula that multiplied the repayment rate (3 percent, 5 percent, or 7 percent, depending on total indebtedness) by the student's AGI in that year. While this self-reliance loan sounds good, incurring an increased future tax liability, rather than a debt, should be of great concern to taxpayers. Therefore, Congress wisely omitted this provision from the final bill.

H.R. 11

While none of the above bills became law, an interesting turn of events occurred during the summer of 1992. Following the violence in Los Angles after the Rodney King verdict, the president and Congress moved swiftly to propose legislation creating enterprise zones.[17] After the House completed its version of this bill, the Senate Finance Committee, chaired by Senator Bentsen, attached additional provisions to the Senate's version of this important bill. Among these additional provisions was much of the education assistance legislation, such as education IRAs, that appeared in S. 612. In addition, all phase-out in the savings bond program based on AGI would be eliminated. While there is no guarantee that this legislation will be enacted, the push for enterprise zones might actually benefit saving for college education.

STATE PROGRAMS

The major action in postsecondary savings programs has occurred at the state level. There are three major types of programs, college savings bonds, prepaid credit programs, and prepaid tuition programs; each has different tax consequences.

College Savings Bonds

The various college savings bond programs are straightforward and uncomplicated.[18] Basically, they involve zero-coupon bonds with stated redemption amounts at maturity (e.g., $5,000). However, the purchase prices of the bonds will vary with the length of maturity (e.g., $900 to $3,500). At maturity, a bond is redeemed at its stated amount, and the difference between its cost and its redemption amount (earnings) is received tax-free.[19] Therefore, college savings bonds are nothing more than municipal bonds that are issued by the state and labeled "college savings bonds."[20] In most cases, the proceeds do not even have to be used for education expenses to gain the tax exemption.

    Although this program is simple, it has two major drawbacks. First, the interest rate earned on municipal bonds takes into account the tax exemption and therefore tends to be much lower than regular market rates of return. Therefore, either it takes longer to earn the amount of money needed, or an individual must invest a greater amount. Second, there is no guarantee that the earnings will cover the rising cost of a college education. This problem of rising costs, and how to project the amount needed, is addressed by the other two types of programs, which offer some form of guaranteed tuition.[21]

Prepaid Credit Programs

In a prepaid credit program, an individual can purchase college credits today, at a set price, to be used in the future. Under Ohio's plan, as an example, each tuition credit is worth 1 percent of the weighted average of the annual cost of tuition at the state's public colleges and universities at the time of redemption. The plan allows parents or other benefactors to purchase up to 400 tuition credits per beneficiary, for use in the future.[22] This allows a family to control the cost of tuition for a student's future college education. For example, parents could purchase 400 college credits today at $35 per credit; the total cost would be $14,000. If the tuition at Ohio State University 15 years later, when the student is ready for college, is $42,000, the student's total tuition cost would be covered. The student could redeem one-fourth of the purchased credits each year as full payment of tuition. While this plan seems uncomplicated, it raises at least three tax questions.

First, when a parent or other benefactor purchases credits for a student, the transaction may be considered a gift for tax purposes.[23] If this is considered to be a gift of a future interest, the annual $10,000 exclusion would not be available.[24] While there is no judicial decision that directly addresses the issue, the Internal Revenue Service (IRS) has ruled that the purchase of tuition credits is a gift of a future interest if the beneficiary has no right to use the funds currently.[25] The Ohio Tuition Trust Authority (OTTA), by its own terms, restricts the use of its tuition credits for at least two years.[26] Therefore, the beneficiary has no right to current use of the credits. However, three additional avenues may exist to assist in this regard:

1. If a parent purchases the credits, the parent might claim that the purchase is not a gift, but the fulfillment of a legal responsibility for providing education to one's children.[27] Other purchasers of the credits would not be able to use this argument.
2. The purchaser could argue that the payment for the credits is covered by Code Section 2503(e)(2)(A), which provides an exception from the classification as a gift for any amount paid on behalf of an individual as

tuition to an education organization. While the tuition payments in a prepaid plan are not going directly to an education organization, the taxpayer might be successful in claiming the "substance-over-form" argument so often used by the IRS.[28]

3. The taxpayer might argue that the payment price for the credits by a purchaser is in the nature of a deposit for the benefit of the beneficiary. If the beneficiary fails to attend college the payment, as well as interest, will be refunded.[29]

The second question arises when the student redeems the tuition credit. If one credit was purchased for $35 but costs $105 on the date of redemption, the redeemer has received a benefit worth $70. Basic tax law provides that the $70 is income, which must be included in the redeeming individual's (i.e., student's) gross income in the year of redemption. The difference between the cost of the credit and its value at redemption is taxable to the redeemer.[30] This difference is the amount that S. 2159 would have excluded from gross income under certain conditions, as discussed earlier. However, at present this amount is taxable.

The third question involves the tax consequences of the investment earnings of the authority that sponsors the program (which in most cases is the state or an integral part of the state). Do the earnings of the sponsoring authority constitute taxable income to the authority, or are they exempt? Taxation of the earnings would decrease the rate of return to the authority, thereby increasing the purchase price of the credits. On the other hand, if the earnings are allowed to grow tax-free, the return to the authority would be increased, and the purchase price of the credits could be lower. Sponsors take the position that these earnings are exempt from taxation, pursuant to Code Section 115, which states, "gross income does not include income derived from any public utility or the exercise of any essential governmental function and accruing to a state or any political subdivision thereof."

The sponsoring authorities believe that the income earned on their investments should be exempt from tax under Section 115, because such income is derived by the authorities in the performance of an essential governmental function that accrues to the benefit of the state. In addition, the authorities have also made the argument that the income earned on the investments should be exempt from federal income taxation pursuant to the doctrine of intergovernmental tax immunity, because the authorities are state instrumentalities. On March 30, 1990, OTTA requested the IRS to rule on these points, but by December 1992, the IRS has yet to reply.[31] In addition to requesting a revenue ruling, OTTA is also lobbying Congress to amend Section 115 to include in its exemption the income earned by state-created tuition trusts.[32]

Prepaid Tuition Programs

The third type of state program, in which most of the tax controversy has occurred, is the prepaid tuition program, such as the Michigan Education Trust (MET)[33] and the Florida Prepaid College Program (FPCP).[34] Under these programs, the purchaser makes a single payment (or installment payments), and four years of college tuition at one of the state's colleges or universities is guaranteed. For example, in 1990, a parent of a newborn child could purchase four years of guaranteed tuition at any Michigan state college, for $8,380.

Before selling its first contract, MET was required to obtain a ruling from the IRS stating that during the administration of the program, the income earned by MET would not be taxed to either the purchaser or the beneficiary. Although the IRS ruled in Michigan's favor, other taxable events were exposed.[35]

These taxable events are very similar to the points raised above in the discussion of prepaid credit programs. However, some of the outcomes may be different. On the issue of taxable income to the beneficiary when the education services are received, there is little argument. The IRS states that the excess of the fair market value of the education services, when received under the contract, over the payment for the contract, is includable in the gross income of the beneficiary or the refund designee. The next issue involves the question of a gift by the purchaser of the contract to the beneficiary. The ruling clearly states that a gift has been made, and that the two possible exceptions were not available in this case.[36] Since the payment was not made directly to an education institution, the Code Section 2503(e)(2)(A) exclusion would fail. In addition, since this transfer was, in fact, a gift of a future interest, the Code Section 2503(b) $10,000-per-year exclusion would also fail. While there is little chance that any purchaser of one of these contracts would have to actually pay any gift tax, each such purchaser would be required to file a gift tax return in the year the contract was purchased or payments were made on behalf of the contract. In fact, like OTTA, MET has been forthright about this fact and has informed its purchasers of this requirement, in some cases forwarding the necessary tax forms.

The final tax issue, which is the most disputed, involves the question of the taxability of the trust's income. In its request for an IRS ruling, MET stated that it believed that since the income earned by the trust during the administration of the program was income earned by an integral part of the state, that income was therefore excluded from gross income. In the alternative, MET stated that the income was derived from the exercise of an essential government function that accrues to the state and should be excluded from gross income under Code Section 115. In response, the IRS recognized that income earned by an integral part of a state or a political subdivision of a state is generally not taxable. However, the IRS also found the facts indicated that MET was not an integral part of the state of Michigan or one of its political subdivisions. In addition, the IRS ruled that even if the income of the trust served a public interest (which is necessary for exemption under Section 115), nontaxable status could be maintained only if any service of a private interest was incidental to service of that public interest. The IRS found that in the case of MET, the private interest served (education payments to beneficiaries of purchased contracts) was more than incidental to the public interest (an educated society) and therefore failed the Section 115 test. Therefore, the income earned by the trust during the administration of the program was includable in the trust's gross income, and subject to federal income tax.[37]

Clearly unhappy with the outcome of the results concerning the trust income question, Michigan and MET decided to file suit against the federal government.[38] The trust filed its tax return (filing as a corporation),[39] paid the tax on the earnings, and filed for a refund. When the refund was denied, the suit was filed. The sole issue revolved around the taxability of the income of the trust during administration of the program.

The state and MET made six arguments in support of exempting MET from taxation:

1. MET is not an entity that is taxable under the provisions of the Code because it is an agency of the sovereign state of Michigan.[40]
2. The United States is prohibited by the modern constitutional doctrine of intergovernmental tax immunity from imposing an income tax on the state of Michigan and MET.[41]

3. The United States is prohibited from imposing an income tax on the state of Michigan and MET because the imposition is discriminatory in its application and is also in violation of the constitutional doctrine of intergovernmental tax immunity.[42]

4. The United States is prohibited from imposing an income tax on the state of Michigan and MET by the Guarantee Clause of the United States Constitution.[43]

5. If the Code were held to be applicable to MET, MET's income is properly excludable from gross income under Code Section 115.[44]

6. If the Code were held to be applicable to MET and MET's income is not excludable under Code Section 115, MET is an organization entitled to recognition as a tax-exempt entity under either Code Section 501(c)(3) or Code Section 501(c)(4).[45]

These theories are alternative pleading at its best. As expected, the federal government disagreed with each of these arguments.[46] The federal government asserted that MET's income is not excludable under Code Section 115,[47] nor does federal taxation of the trust's income violate any constitutional protections or run afoul of intergovernmental tax immunity or the nondiscrimination doctrine.[48] In addition, as stated in the IRS reply to MET's request for tax-exempt status under Code Section 501(c)(3) or 501(c)(4), MET did not qualify as a tax-exempt charitable organization.[49]

The decision in this case was rendered on July 28, 1992.[50] In denying plaintiff's motion for summary judgment and granting defendant's motion for summary judgment, Justice Douglas W. Hillman agreed with the federal government on each argument. As to the statutory argument made by MET that it was not subject to the Internal Revenue Code because the Code was not intended to apply to states or their instrumentalities, the court stated:

> This argument fails because MET is not an integral part of the state of Michigan. The Code does not contain any provision expressly stating that it does not apply to states. Rather, states have *de facto* exemption from the Code because the Code, by its terms, applies only to individuals and entities such as corporations. Congress never intended the Code to apply to the states. Whatever its relationship to the state, the MET is a corporation to which the Code, by its terms, applies. The question, then, is whether the MET is also an integral part of the state of Michigan entitled to the state's *de facto* immunity.

I conclude that the MET is not an integral part of the state of Michigan. While the MET received its start-up funds from the state, the funds out of which it provides its tuition-guaranteeing service come from contracts with private individuals, not from the state. The state may not use MET's funds to pay creditors of the state, nor may the state use the MET's funds for any other purposes. Conversely, while the act provides that MET may contract with subscribers "on behalf of itself and the state," it was conceded at oral argument that Michigan does not back up those contracts with its full faith and credit. These facts all demonstrate that MET is an entity distinct from the state. Therefore, the MET is subject to the Code.[51]

Addressing the Code Section 115 concern,[52] the court approached the question in two ways. First, its determination that MET was not an integral part of the state disposed of the argument that Section 115 directly alters the tax status of MET. Second, the court closely examined the "accrual" requirement. Citing *City of Woodway v. United States*[53] and *City of Bethel v. United States,*[54] the court concluded that, for purposes of Section 115, "income accrues to a state only when some kind of actual or bookkeeping transfer of funds occurs.[55] In essence, the state or political subdivision of the state must have some "vested right" or "enforceable claim" to the income.[56] With regard to MET, the court finding that the accrual requirement was lacking stated:

> The act provides that Michigan has no claim to MET's assets, including the investment income. As noted above, MET's funds may not be considered "common cash" of the state, nor may they be considered "state money." Michigan may not use the money to pay the obligations of the state. No actual or booking transfer of funds to the state occurs. The only situation in which Michigan would have any such vested right would occur in the event that the trust were dissolved because of an actual unsoundness and assets were left over after paying creditors and distributing pro rata benefits to subscribers. In short, Michigan presently has no "vested right" or "enforceable claim" to MET's investment income. In the language of the Code, MET's income does not "accrue" to the state. Therefore, Section 115 does not provide an exemption for MET's income.[57]

The last statutory argument presented by MET, involving its exemption pursuant to Code Section 501(c)(3)[58] or Code Section 501(c)(4),[59] also failed. Although both parties agree that the presence of a substantial

nonexempt purpose will destroy an organization's exemption, they differ
on the extent of MET's exempt purpose and private purpose. MET asserts
that the private benefits gained by the purchasers of MET contracts are
only incidental to the public benefits gained by society at large—having a
well-educated populace. The government contends that the private benefit is so substantial that it prevents exemption under Code Section
501(c)(3) or Code Section 501(c)(4). In holding for the government on
this point, Justice Hillman said:

> In my view, the trust's purpose of providing the tuition guaranteeing
> service constitutes a substantial private purpose that destroys the trust's
> exemption. I arrive at this conclusion primarily because the trust's sole
> direct benefit inures only to individuals who purchase contracts. Ac-
> cordingly, I conclude that MET does not qualify for exemption under
> Sections 501(c)(3) and 501(c)(4) of the code.[60]

In regard to the constitutional concerns, the court also responded to
each one separately. On the issue alleging that the federal government's
tax on MET violated the Guarantee Clause of the U.S. Constitution, the
court's response was swift and brief. Citing *Luther v. Boden*[61] and *Baker v.
Carr*,[62] the court followed the Supreme Court direction that the Guarantee Clause does not provide judicially manageable standards and therefore
is nonjusticiable. In so doing, the court rejected MET's request to follow
Justice O'Connor's dissent in *South Carolina v. Baker*,[63] in which she argued that judicial enforcement of the Guarantee Clause is proper.

MET's argument that the Tenth Amendment[64] to the U.S. Constitution prohibits imposition of the tax was also rejected by the court. Recognizing that the Tenth Amendment sets only "structural limits," not
substantive limits, on congressional authority to regulate state activities,
the court explained that "states must find their protection from congressional regulation through the national political process, not through judicially defined spheres of unregulable state activity."[65] The court found
that MET did not fit the requirements of either of the two exceptions to
this rule; MET did not show that (1) an extraordinary defect in the national political process led to the adoption of the Code or (2) the imposition of the tax interferes with core concerns fundamentally related to the
sovereign nature of the state of Michigan. The court suggested that MET
and the state of Michigan seek protection not from the courts, but from
Congress.

In resolving the doctrine of intergovernmental tax immunity, the court, recognizing that the doctrine holds that states are constitutionally immune from federal taxation, addresses two concerns. First, can the United States ever impose a tax directly on the states or on parties with whom the states deal? Second, if the federal government can tax the states or an entity that deals with the states, does the imposition of such a tax have the effect of discriminating against the states in favor of the federal government?

In addressing the first question in the affirmative, the court stated:

> Under current intergovernmental tax immunity doctrine, the United States can tax any private parties with whom a state does business, even though the financial burden falls on the state, so long as the tax does not discriminate against the state, or those with whom it deals, in favor of the federal government. *South Carolina v. Baker,* 485 U.S. at 523. In addition, at least some nondiscriminatory federal taxes can be collected directly from the states even though a parallel state tax could not be collected directly from the federal government. *Id.* A tax is considered to be directly "on" the state only when the levy falls on the state itself, "or on an agency or instrumentality so closely connected to the government that the two cannot realistically be viewed as separate entities." *Id.,* 485 U.S. at 519 N.11, 523 (quoting *United States v. New Mexico,* 455 U.S. 720, 735 (1981)).

Stating the doctrine in this way, in light of this court's earlier determination that the trust is not an integral part of the state, disposes of the issue of whether the trust could ever legitimately be subject to federal taxation. The trust's status as an entity established by the state of Michigan does not implicate the doctrine because the trust is not so closely connected to the state that the two cannot realistically be viewed as separate entities.[66]

In addressing the second question, the court found problems with portions of both parties' arguments. Recognizing that the dispute centered on which entities constitute appropriate standards of comparison by which to measure discrimination, the court partially rejected both MET's argument that the comparison should be made with a variety of federal and state agencies, and the government's argument that the comparison should be with other providers of investment services, such as banks. Accepting portions of both parties' arguments, the court stated that the comparison group should consist of entities created by the federal government that provide some sort of investment service similar to that which the trust provides. Having established the level of comparison, the court found that none of the federally created entities and programs identified by MET were sufficiently similar to the trust to fit within the comparison made; therefore the court held that the discrimination portion of the doctrine of intergovernmental tax immunity should not apply. While each of the federal programs identified by MET permitted investment of funds to support the goals of the program, these programs differed substantially from MET, in that the federal programs did not function primarily as an investment service for their individual beneficiaries. The court found that MET's investment services were primarily for its individual beneficiaries. Noting this, the court felt that the differing tax treatments given MET and other federal programs did not violate the doctrine of intergovernmental tax immunity.

MET's judicial defeat appears to signal that the responses to the ruling request made by Ohio and that made by Florida in April 1990 will be negative. However, as discussed in Chapter 4, Florida contends that its prepaid tuition plan is so substantially different from MET that it warrants different treatment. In essence, Florida believes that its trust is not a separate entity but an integral part of the state; that it provides an essential government function; and that it is backed by the full faith and credit of the state of Florida.

One lingering question remains: are the funds collected by FPPEEP subject to other creditors of the state of Florida? Although Florida is hoping for a positive response to its ruling request, it is probable that if the ruling is in fact negative, the state of Florida and its trust will test the judicial waters.[67]

THE PRIVATE SECTOR

Of course, families can attempt to provide for the future cost of higher education without the benefit of any assistance by the federal or state governments. In fact, there is plenty of help available in other areas. Insurance companies are willing to show how annuity contracts and cash-value life insurance can provide money for future education costs. While they are correct that the income builds up tax-free, one must be concerned about the rate of return and the tax consequences on distribution. Additionally, the security of the insurance industry itself must be considered.

Brokerage houses are also ready to assist. It is common knowledge that over time, nothing outpaces the stock market; however, stocks have various degrees of risk, dividends are taxable, and certain gains on the sale of any stock will clearly produce taxable income. Of course, families can buy tax-free municipal bonds that mature over the four-year period during which their children will be attending college; the income earned will be tax-free under Code Section 103. However, many states provide the same advantages through their education savings bonds, and don't charge a brokerage commission.

There are private companies and banks that sell different types of plans to help families meet the ever-increasing costs. One such company is the College Savings Bank of Princeton, New Jersey, which offers a "CollegeSure CD" whose interest rate changes each year to match escalating college costs.[68] While these plans are a little more flexible as to the choice of colleges than state plans, the tax aspects of each should be carefully considered.

Employers have also entered the arena. RJR Nabisco has created a program of loans, scholarships, and up to $4,000 of matching funds, in an effort to assist its employees.[69] RJR Nabisco has stated that no child of an RJR Nabisco employee will be denied a college education because of lack of money.

Many magazines, such as *Money, Newsweek,* and *Black Enterprise,* publish articles on how to save for college. Most suggest such vehicles as passbook accounts, mutual funds, CDs, bonds, custodial accounts, and ownership of rental real estate. However, all of these have tax aspects that must be taken into account. In addition, returns on many of these vehicles fell below the rate of inflation in 1992.

There is no question that providing for future higher education costs has reached a complex level. I myself have purchased U.S. Savings Bonds, tuition credits, municipal bonds, mutual funds, a Section 403(b) account, and rental real estate, and also hope to benefit from discount tuition provisions because I am employed by Ohio State University; however, I am still searching for the best plan.

NOTES

1. David Williams II, "Financing a College Education: A Taxing Dilemma," *Ohio State Law Journal* 50(1989):561.

2. See, for example, Robert W. McLeod and William D. Samson, "College Planning: Hitting the Mark; The World of Financial Planning," which cites a Department of Education study that estimates that 18 years from now, four years at a private college that now cost $50,000 will cost $200,000, and at a public college, currently $18,600, will cost $60,000.

   Newsweek, in its October 21, 1991, article entitled "How to Save for College" by Jane Bryant Quinn, estimates that by 2008, four years at a private college will cost $250,000, whereas four years at an in-state public college will cost $120,000.

3. See Section 117 of the Internal Revenue Code of 1986 (hereafter, Code), which exempts from taxation only the portion of a scholarship that meets the requirements of a "qualified scholarship." Under Section 117(b), a qualified scholarship includes those amounts used for "qualified tuition and related expenses," which are defined as tuition and fees required for enrollment or attendance; and fees, books, supplies, and equipment required for courses of instruction. Scholarship funds used for other expenses, such as room and board are, therefore, subject to federal taxation.

4. See Code Section 163, which allows the deduction of some types of interest paid. However, interest paid on student loans is considered personal interest and is therefore nondeductible, pursuant to Section 163(h).

5. Code Section 135(a).

6. Code Section 135(b)(1).

7. See *Tax Bulletin, Federal Taxes* 2nd Vol. 43, October 24, 1991, which discusses how to build a college fund using EE Savings Bonds.

8. Code Section 135(c)(1).

9. Code Section 135(c)(2).

10. Code Section 135(b)(2).

11. S. 612, 102nd Cong., 1st Sess. (1991).

12. On July 31, 1991, the author testified before the Senate Finance Committee regarding this bill. See "Hearing Before the Committee on Finance, United States Senate, 102nd Congress, First Session on S. 612, July 31, 1991."

13. S. 2159, 102nd Cong., 2nd Sess. (1992).

14. This provision removed the limitation imposed by Code Section 163, as described in note 4.

15. As described in note 3.

16. For example, the Michigan Education Trust, the Ohio Tuition Trust, and the Florida Prepaid College Program, all to be discussed later.

17. H.R. 11, 102nd Cong., 2nd Sess. (1992). The concept of enterprise zones is beyond the scope of this chapter. See David Williams II, "The Enterprise Zone Concept at the Federal Level. Are Proposed Tax Incentives the Needed Ingredient?" *Virginia Tax Review* 9(1990):711 for a discussion.

18. See Chapter 1 of this volume for a complete listing of plans.

19. See Code Section 103, which allows the proceeds from municipal bonds to escape federal taxation.

20. These bonds are actually general obligation bonds issued by the state authority.

21. While Alabama, Alaska, Florida, Indiana, Louisiana, Maine, Michigan, Missouri, Ohio, Oklahoma, West Virginia, and Wyoming have adopted such plans, only Florida, Michigan, Ohio, and Wyoming have implemented their plans.

22. The Ohio Tuition Trust Authority (OTTA) oversees the Ohio Tuition Trust Plan, which was signed into law on July 1, 1989. Ohio Rev. Code Ann. Section 3334(A). The weighted average tuition represents the average tuition paid by all students at the 13 Ohio public colleges and universities. It is calculated by multiplying the enrollment at each of the 13 Ohio public institutions by the tuition and mandatory fees paid at that institution, and dividing the result by the total enrollment at all 13 institutions.

23. Code Section 2501 imposes a tax on a donor who makes a transfer of property by gift.

24. Pursuant to Code Section 2503(b), the first $10,000 of such gifts, other than gifts of future interest in property, made by a donor during the calendar year, gifts to such person shall not be included in the total amount of gifts made during the year.

25. Priv. Ltr. Rul. 88-25-027 (March 29, 1988). For further discussion of this issue, see Williams, "Financing a College Education."

26. Ohio's program actually informs its purchasers that the purchase of credits does constitute a gift, and that individual purchasers must file the necessary annual gift tax returns. However, in most cases, due to the gift tax unified credit (see Code Section 2505), very few individuals will actually be required to pay any gift tax.

27. If parents provide only what they are legally responsible to provide, there is no gift.

28. This doctrine, a longstanding element in tax law, states that the substance of any transaction, regardless of its form, dictates its tax consequences.

29. This principle reflects the theory that a gift has to be completed at the time of purchase of the credits. However, the government, referring to the Ohio program, rejects this argument on two grounds. First, the powers retained by the purchaser can be exercised only with the consent of the beneficiary, a person whose interest is substantially adverse to the interest of the purchaser. *Commissioner v. Prouty*, U.S.T.C., 115 F.2d 331 (1st Cir. 1940). Second, even if the interest of the beneficiary was not considered adverse, the purchaser has retained only the possibility for reversion, and a possibility of reversion does not prevent a gift from being complete. *Smith v. Shaughnessy* 318 U.S. 176 (1943).

30. Code Sections 61(a) and 1001.

31. On July 28, 1992, the Western District of Michigan Federal District Court decided the case of *State of Michigan, and its Michigan Education Trust v. United States of America*, No. 5:90-cv-35, 1992 U.S. Dist. LEXIS 12258 (W.D. Mich. July 28, 1992), (hereafter, *Michigan v. U.S.*). The court decided in favor of the government. It is the author's belief that because of this decision, the response to OTTA's request will be negative.

32. The desired amendment would state that gross income does not include "Income received by or accruing to a trust, fund, or similar organization created or organized by

a state for the purpose of operating a prepaid tuition or education expense program for the benefit of the state's residents."

33. Michigan Education Trust, Mich. Comp. Laws Section 390.1421 (1991).

34. Florida Prepaid Postsecondary Education Expense Program, Fla. Stat. ch. 240.551 (1991).

35. Priv. Ltr. Rul. 88-25-027 (March 29, 1988).

36. Ibid.

37. Ibid.

38. *Michigan v. U.S.* It should be noted that Michigan discontinued the selling of MET contracts shortly before this action. There is dispute as to the reason; various observers have ascribed it to the negative revenue ruling, faulty projections, or a political ploy by the new Republican governor to upstage the former Democratic leadership.

39. Although MET was labeled a trust, under tax law this title is not determinative for tax purposes. In fact, if an entity has characteristics that suggest that it more resembles some other type of entity, it will be classified as that other entity for tax purposes, regardless of its legal title. See Code Section 7701(a)(3); Treas. Regulation Sections 301.7701-1 and 301.7701-2; *Morrissey et al. v. Commissioner*, 296 U.S. 344 (1935). Based on these standards, MET was designated a corporation for tax purposes.

40. See Brief in Support of Motion for Summary Judgment by the state of Michigan and its Michigan Education Trust, filed October 25, 1991.

41. Ibid. The substance of MET's argument under this theory revolves around a two-step approach: first, under the doctrine of intergovernmental tax immunity, the states and the federal government are not supposed to tax one another, under the premise of protecting traditional governmental functions; and second, MET is in fact an innovative tool to promote the traditional state function of education.

42. Ibid. MET argues that the federal government taxes it, but does not tax other similarly situated agencies that provide essential functions, such as the federal student loan program, federal insurance programs, the Federal Deposit Insurance Corporation, the United States Postal Service, local and state bus services, and state housing authorities.

43. Ibid. Under this theory, MET argues that by taxing the trust, the federal government is interfering with the state's autonomy. It should be noted that in its brief, MET requested that the court consider this a matter appropriate for judicial review.

44. Ibid. Here, MET uses the Section 115 analysis to compare the similarities between MET's prepaid tuition program and a railroad (see Alaska Railroad Transfer Act, 45 U.S.C. Sections 1201 et seq.) that benefits from Section 115. MET argues that its income accrues to the state either by way of state universities or by discharging obligations owed by MET on behalf of the state. With regard to the required essential government function, MET contends that it provides a public service that does not benefit individuals, but benefits the community as a whole by encouraging education. Further, MET questions the government's interpretation that a public purpose cannot coexist with private purposes.

45. Ibid. Finally, MET claims that it should be granted an exemption from taxation under Code Section 501(c)(3). MET asserts that it is a charitable/educational entity, in which no net earnings accrue to any private individual. Although admitting that an individual may benefit from the program, it asserts that this occurs only in that individual's status as a member of the community as a whole. In addition, MET believes it meets Section 501(c)(4) exemption requirements, since it is an organization for the social welfare of the community, not a limited group.

46. See Brief for the Defendant in Support of its Motion for Summary Judgment by the United States Government, filed December 23, 1991.

47. Ibid. The federal government claims that MET does not perform an essential government function because of its large benefit to private individuals instead of the community as a whole. In addition, the government asserts that no income accrues to the state, not even constructively, because the money is funneled back to the beneficiaries.

48. Ibid. Although the government concedes that MET was created by the legislature and is subject to state regulations, it contends that MET is not directly controlled by the state. Therefore, the government asserts that MET is not a state entity, agency, or instrumentality. Furthermore, the government argues that the doctrine of intergovernmental tax immunity has been limited in recent years so that the federal government can tax a state unless the tax interferes with an essential governmental function that cannot be performed by a private entity.

49. Ibid. As to the charitable-organization argument, the government contends that MET fails both the organizational and operational tests under Code Section 501(c)(3). See Treas. Regulations Section 1.501(c)(3)-1. The government further argues that although MET serves a public purpose, it also serves a substantial nonexempt purpose of providing individuals with financial benefits.

50. *State of Michigan v. United States*, 802 F. Supp. 120 (W.D. Mich. 1992).

51. Ibid. See generally D. Richardson, "Federal Income Taxation of States," *Stetson Law Review* 19 (1990):411; Michigan Compiled Laws Annotated 390, 1429(2) and Michigan Compiled Laws Annotated 390, 1437.

52. Code Section 115 states, "Gross income does not include (1) income derived from ... the exercise of any essential governmental function and accruing to a state or any political subdivision thereof."

53. *City of Woodway v. United States*, 681 F.2nd 975, 980 (5th Cir. 1982).

54. *City of Bethel v. United States*, 594 F.2d 1301 (9th Cir. 1979).

55. *Michigan v. U.S.*

56. Ibid. The court cited *Omaha Public Power District v. O'Malley*, 232 F.2d 805, 809 (8th Cir.), *cert. denied*, 352 U.S. 837 (1956); *Troy State Univ. v. Commissioner*, 62 T.C. 493, 497 (1974).

57. *Michigan v. U.S.*

58. Code Section 501(c)(3) exempts from taxation those organizations "organized and operated exclusively for ... charitable ... or education purposes, ... no part of the net earnings of which inures to the benefit of any private shareholder or individual."

59. Code Section 501(c)(4) exempts "organizations not organized for profit but operated exclusively for the promotion of social welfare."

60. *Michigan v. U.S.*

61. *Luther v. Boden*, 48 U.S. (7 How.) 1,42 (1849).

62. 369 U.S. 186, 218-232 (1962); 82 S. Ct. 691, 710-718 (1962), *on remand* 206 F. Supp. 341 (M.D. Tenn. 1962).

63. 485 U.S. 505 (1988).

64. The Tenth Amendment states, "The powers not delegated to the United States by the Constitution, nor prohibited by it to the states, are reserved to the states respectively, or to the people."

65. *Michigan v. U.S.* The court cites *South Carolina v. Baker*, 485 U.S. 505, 512 (1988), which cites *Garcia v. San Antonio Metropolitan Transit Authority*, 469 U.S. 528 (1985).

66. *Michigan v. U.S.*

67. As this book went to press, the IRS had ruled that the Kentucky Education Savings Plan Trust was ineligible for tax-exempt status due to the way its investments were pooled. Nonetheless, the state intends to continue the program. See "A Decision by the Internal Revenue Service," *Chronicle of Higher Education* (July 14, 1993).

68. See "CDs Pegged to College Costs Look Good to Parents, but Do They Make the Grade?" *Wall Street Journal* (March 20, 1992):C1.

69. See "RJR Nabisco Plan Would Help Pay College Costs of Employees' Children," *Chronicle of Higher Education* (March 11, 1992):A.28.

Chapter 6

Real-Return Investments as a Tuition Hedge

Lewis J. Spellman

The quest for the "risk-free lunch" has been extended to college tuition. The Michigan Education Trust (MET) and other similar prepaid college tuition plans (CTPs) have justifiably caused their advocates to be proud of their adoption. But now that these programs are actually being implemented, some doubts are beginning to arise.[1] The significant question is: should society be pleased or worried if the CTP sells well in the marketplace? We must consider the possibility that an embarrassing potential for bankruptcy may have been created.

POTENTIAL PROBLEMS

If a plan sells well, there are two likely reasons. First, the plan may be underpriced (its prepaid tuition fee is too low). The underpricing may result from unrealistic assumptions regarding the ability of the fund's assets to realize returns greater than the rate of inflation over the long haul. This would eventually lead to the plan's bankruptcy, when it could not pay its obligations. Such a bankruptcy would cause a future legislature to be faced with the necessity for either a repudiation or a bailout. A bailout

Lewis J. Spellman is professor of finance at the University of Texas, and chairman of Real Rate Financial in Austin.

would result in intergenerational wealth transfers, adversely affecting all residents with what in effect had become a statewide college scholarship program. This intergenerational wealth transfer, paid through general taxation, would put a damper on the state's economic activity. A repudiation would result in an obvious net loss to all purchasers, and might well deny a college education to beneficiaries.

The second reason a CTP might do well in the marketplace is the perceived reduction in financial risk for parents wishing to fund a college education. Without a CTP, such parents would have to organize their own investment programs, and hope that the returns would be sufficient to generate the necessary future income to pay college tuition. MET and other CTPs appear to provide the comfort of shifting the risk of an unsuccessful investment program to a state-sponsored agency. In exchange for avoiding this risk, parents would probably elect a CTP even if it promised a lower expected return than their own investment programs.[2]

Participation in a CTP shifts the financial risk to the state-sponsored agency and future legislators and taxpayers (even if there is only an implicit guarantee by the state on the CTP's obligations). This chapter analyzes the financial risk that the CTPs (and future taxpayers) have accepted, and the ability of the CTPs to make good on their promises.

CTPs have much in common with federal programs that have arisen out of a concern for providing goods or services considered to have substantial social benefit. For example, the need to provide affordable housing has led the federal government to create government-sponsored financing and government insurance programs. Because these programs accept fees currently but pay benefits many years later, a bankruptcy might not be obvious for some time, but it is incumbent on all involved to take a hard look at the obligations that have been made and make corrections at an early stage, rather than when the obligations are due. The same precautions apply to CTPs.

ANALOGY TO BANKS

One analysis of MET's financial risk uses an analogy to a bank.[3] The analogy is quite appropriate for all CTPs, so let us examine a hypothetical "CTP Bank." The CTP Bank is very special in that it accepts deposits with a very long maturity but pays no current interest; all interest is accrued until the time of withdrawal. This makes its deposits the equivalent of zero-coupon instruments. Technically speaking, the deposit maturities of the bank's obligations are long-term—possibly up to 30 years in some programs—but these maturities are not completely fixed, since there is a window of time during which the funds could be withdrawn. There is a very substantial penalty for early withdrawals, typically involving the loss of interest (sometimes many years of accumulated interest). Further discounting of the deposits occurs if they are "put" back to the CTP Bank in the case that the beneficiary does not attend college at all, or attends a private college, or perhaps attends a college in another state. These "put" discounts on the claims are an important offset to the obligations faced by the CTP Bank.

Although these conditions would be relatively standard, manageable, and potentially profitable in ordinary banking, what sets the CTP Bank apart from conventional banks is that the amount of the bank's obligations or liability is not set by the bank. Rather, it is indexed to the prices in a service industry of which the bank has no prior knowledge or control, and in recent years the prices in that service industry have been increasing more rapidly than the overall price index. This raises the crucial question of whether the bank will be able to honor its obligations in the future, if its returns on long-term, high-grade investment portfolios do not systematically exceed the inflation rate.

The ability to systematically beat the inflation rate is the risk that has been shifted to the CTPs. They, in turn, must seek to shift that risk to those entities able to do so. This risk shifting can be accomplished by acquiring a portfolio of real rate- or inflation-adjusting financial assets.

THE CTP BANK'S PROMISE

A bank may promise a specified return, but fulfilling that promise may be difficult. The college-tuition component of the Consumer Price Index (CPI) has been increasing at a rate of 9.1 percent per annum during the 1970s and 1980s. During the same period, the overall CPI increased by 6.3 percent annually.[4] Thus, the CTP Bank's obligations would have had to grow about 2.8 percent faster than the CPI. The amount by which college tuition outpaces overall inflation might be referred to as the "real tuition growth rate."

Over shorter periods of time, such as between 1986 and 1990, the CPI for educational service as well as tuition per full-time equivalent student outpaced the overall CPI, resulting in a 4 percent real increase in the 1980s and a 3.1 percent increase in 1988-90. Both the rate of inflation and the margin by which tuition outpaced overall inflation were substantial. To the CTP Bank, its beneficiaries, and the taxpayers, the warning flags are out. There is a serious question of the CTP Bank's ability to service its liabilities if these liabilities continue to grow at such high absolute rates and at such high rates relative to the CPI's rate of increase.

The reason for concern is that the real tuition growth rate must be equaled by the CTP Bank's investment portfolio if it is to meet its obligations. Thus, the CTP Bank's portfolio in 1986 to 1990 would have had to earn returns that exceeded 3 percent in real terms.[5]

The problem for the CTP Bank is that financial markets often do not generate earnings even equal to the CTPI rate of increase, let alone produce real growth rates of 3 percent over a lengthy period of time. Although rapid growth rates in financial performance sometimes occur, there is no guarantee that the timing of returns on financial markets would match the timing required by the CTP Bank to satisfy its obligations.

In essence, the ability to deliver on the CTP Bank's promise hinges on a consistent long-term performance of its portfolio. Its portfolio managers must earn real rates of return on investments that generate consistent and positive real yields of approximately 3 percent. Long-term *average* performance is not enough. This is the problem facing the CTP Bank, and this is the risk it has accepted. Table 6.1 shows the inflation-adjusted returns for overlapping 20-year periods for stocks, long-term corporate and government bonds, and short-term government bills. Such results are not easily achieved, because the earnings of investments in financial markets often do not exceed inflation rates. If anything, acceleration of inflation typically causes real portfolio returns to decline, possibly for a decade or more. This is true for long-term debt instruments and sometimes also for equities.

THE RATE OF TUITION INFLATION

College fees have not only increased, but have increased at a rate that exceeds the overall inflation rate for two decades. While we cannot examine the causes here, a few observations are appropriate.

When the price of a good increases relative to that of other goods, this

Table 6.1. Compounded Annual Real Returns for 20-Year Periods (1961–1988)

Time Period	Common Stocks (%)	Long-Term Corporate Bonds (%)	Long-Term Government Bonds (%)	Short-Term Government Bonds (%)
1961-1980	2.85	−2.12	−2.87	.05
1962-1981	.89	−2.82	−3.23	.25
1963-1982	2.29	−1.47	−1.97	.50
1964-1983	2.16	−1.46	−2.10	.68
1965-1984	1.53	−1.04	−1.68	.86
1966-1985	2.30	.31	− .39	.95
1967-1986	3.93	1.39	.70	1.14
1968-1987	2.96	1.58	1.00	1.13
1969-1988	3.24	2.00	1.52	1.20

Source: R.S. Ibbotson and R.A. Sinquefield, *Stocks, Bonds, Bills and Inflation, 1988 Quarterly Market Reports* (Chicago: Ibbotson Associates, 1988); J. Teek and J. Wilcox, "A Real, Affordable Mortgage," *New England Economics Review* (January/February 1991), p. 51.

increase sets off forces that readjust prices in the future. This is simply the mechanism inherent in a market economy, with its freedom of entry by other producers and by labor, and the freedom of demanders to satisfy their education needs more economically. Therefore, long-term price projections based on historical trends are bound to be inaccurate because of these self-adjusting mechanisms.

Since the primary source of tuition inflation is the labor component of college costs, this inaccuracy is to be expected. (This is documented in a study by Arthur Hauptman, *The College Tuition Spiral,* published jointly by ACE and the College Board in 1990.) Long cycles of accelerated inflation may last a minimum of a half decade; the time required to attract and train a prospective faculty member through graduate school is at least five to six years. Over a period of time, higher faculty salaries attract new trainees, whose eventual entry into the market puts downward pressure on faculty pay scales. (This phenomenon is known as a "cobweb cycle.") Pressures for reduced college tuition inflation also exist on the demand side. If college becomes too expensive, there is a moderation of demand, causing the price increases to slow down as college-age students find alternative and less costly training.

Another factor influencing college tuition is the long-term prospect for real growth in wages, which are the largest component of college costs. Any productivity gains in the economy as a whole should be reflected in growing real wages and hence pressures for a real rate of inflation in tuition. That is, basic college wage costs grow at a rate equal to the inflation rate plus the gain in productivity. While one might not think that college professors are capable of achieving productivity gains, if they have nonacademic employment options in a more productive economy, competition for labor will drive up college wages along with industry wages for most disciplines. This economic pressure on professorial wages imposes on the CTP Bank the need to achieve returns that exceed the inflation rate. Long cycles in real wage gains are a source of pressure for the bank's portfolio to produce positive real earnings. Though this has not been a source of pressure on the CTP Bank in the past decade, it might be in the future.

Because of these mechanisms, it is foolhardy to project the historic college tuition growth rate. It could be equal to, be less than, or exceed the CPI, but the CTP Bank must be able to generate positive real returns in its portfolio operations to be prepared for all eventualities.

THE IRONY OF THE PATTERNS OF REAL RETURNS IN FINANCIAL MARKETS

The job of the CTP Bank portfolio manager—to earn returns equal to the tuition inflation rate in order to ensure the survival of the bank as a viable economic entity—is not an easy one. Table 6.1 illustrates the real returns available from the traditional investment outlets for CTP funds—common stocks, corporate or government long-term debt, and short-term government debt. A portfolio manager would probably choose the seemingly less risky long-term debt instruments. However, neither long-term nor short-term bonds have generated consistent 20-year real returns of 3 percent; in fact, in several of these periods they have generated negative real returns. Only common stocks have come close to realizing, over 20-year periods, the 3 percent real rate of inflation in tuition in the past two decades; this occurred in only two of the nine overlapping 20-year holding periods.

Table 6.2. CTP Bank Growth Rate of Assets and Liabilities per Deposit Dollar (1966–1986)

Year	Common Stocks (%)	Short-Term Government Bonds (%)	Long-Term Government Bonds (%)	Liabilities[*] (%)	Inflation Rate[†] (%)
1966	−10.06	4.76	3.65	6.85	3.35
1967	24.98	4.21	−9.19	6.54	3.04
1968	11.06	5.21	−0.26	8.22	4.72
1969	−8.50	6.58	−5.08	9.61	6.11
1970	4.01	6.53	12.10	8.99	5.49
1971	14.31	4.39	13.23	6.86	3.36
1972	18.98	3.84	5.68	6.91	3.41
1973	−14.66	6.93	−1.11	12.30	8.80
1974	−26.47	8.00	4.35	15.70	12.20
1975	37.20	5.80	9.19	10.51	7.01
1976	23.84	5.08	16.75	8.31	4.81
1977	−7.18	5.12	−0.67	10.27	6.77
1978	6.56	7.18	−1.16	12.53	9.03
1979	18.44	10.38	−1.22	16.81	13.31
1980	32.42	11.24	−3.95	15.90	12.40
1981	−4.91	14.71	1.85	12.44	8.94
1982	21.41	10.54	40.35	7.37	3.87
1983	25.51	8.80	0.68	7.30	3.80
1984	6.27	9.85	15.43	7.45	3.95
1985	32.16	7.72	30.97	7.27	3.77
1986	18.47	6.16	24.44	4.63	1.13

[*]Presuming a 3.5 percent real tuition growth rate.

[†]Unadjusted CPI.

Source: J.Teek and J. Wilcox, "A Real, Affordable Mortgage," *New England Economics Review* (January/February 1991), p. 51.

While the equity returns have been reasonable on average, they are less impressive when reviewed in terms of their year-by-year stability. Table 6.2 shows the short-term instability in the total returns of stocks and the other alternative investments, even before correcting for inflation. Total returns take into account not only the current returns of interest payments and dividends, but also the capital gains and losses of the portfolio (as if everything were sold at the end of each year). This is a reality check called "mark-to-market" accounting.

Note that the year-to-year returns are often decidedly negative; this volatility is true for both stocks and long-term debt, whether corporate or government. The reason for these annual losses by debt instruments is that higher inflation rates reduce the purchasing power of long-term, fixed-income debt instruments, causing the bond market to react with lower prices for the outstanding debt issues. This would be true even if the CTP Bank purchased insurance-based contracts such as guaranteed investment contracts (GICs), which are long-term debt instruments.

Hence, although stocks may perform well over the long haul, they do not do so year by year, and it is not likely that a CTP Bank manager would be able to withstand the criticism that would occur in the years in which equities declined in value. The more likely and seemingly defensible investments are the long-term, high-grade corporate and government issues. These, however, are subject to frequent negative long-term real returns as well as high volatility. To make matters worse, the volatility in the returns on long-term debt are systematically negative just when the CTP Bank's liabilities accelerate. That is, if the CTP Bank had an approximate 3.5 percent real tuition growth rate applied to its liabilities, but had invested in the seemingly reasonable category of long-term government bonds, an acceleration of inflation in a given year would substantially increase the bank's liabilities, and the market value of its assets would decline substantially.

The CTP Bank's net worth would be the difference between (1) the appreciation or depreciation of its assets and (2) the growth of its liabilities. The tendency for the CTP Bank's net worth to vary inversely with inflation is shown in Figures 6.1 and 6.2 and in Table 6.3. Both figures assume that the CTP Bank held a portfolio consisting exclusively of long-term government debt. Figure 6.1 compares the growth rates of the bank's assets and liabilities, based on a real tuition growth rate of 3.5 percent. The net effect of the relationship between the growth rates of assets and of liabilities is summarized in Figure 6.2, which shows the change that would have occurred in

Figure 6.1. Growth Rates of Assets and Liabilities (1966–1986)

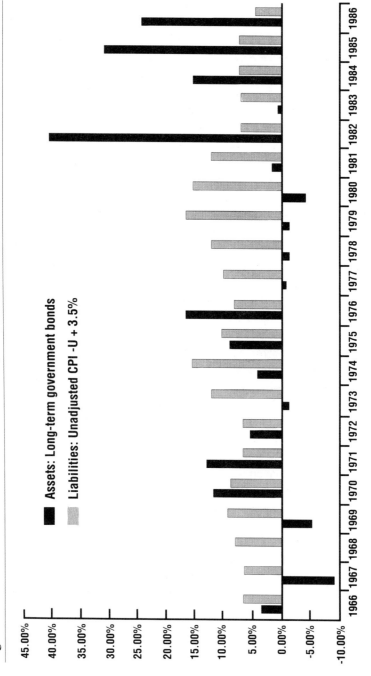

Assets: Long-term government bonds

Liabilities: Unadjusted CPI -U + 3.5%

Source: J. Teek and J. Wilcox, "A Real, Affordable Mortgage," *New England Journal of Economics* (January/February 1991), p. 51

Table 6.3. CTP Bank's Changes in Net Worth (1966–1986)

Year	For Portfolios Of: Common Stocks (%)	Short-Term Government Bonds (%)	Long-Term Government Bonds (%)	Inflation Rate* (%)
1966	−16.91	−2.09	−3.20	3.35
1967	18.44	−2.33	−15.73	3.04
1968	2.84	−3.01	−8.48	4.72
1969	−18.11	−3.03	−14.69	6.11
1970	−4.98	−2.46	3.11	5.49
1971	7.45	−2.47	6.37	3.36
1972	12.07	−3.07	−1.23	3.41
1973	−26.96	−5.37	−13.41	8.80
1974	−42.17	−7.70	−11.35	12.20
1975	26.69	−4.71	−1.32	7.01
1976	15.53	−3.23	8.44	4.81
1977	−17.45	−5.15	−10.94	6.77
1978	−5.97	−5.35	−13.69	9.03
1979	1.63	−6.43	−18.03	13.31
1980	16.52	−4.66	−19.85	12.40
1981	−17.35	2.27	−10.59	8.94
1982	14.04	3.17	32.98	3.87
1983	18.21	1.50	−6.62	3.80
1984	−1.18	2.40	7.98	3.95
1985	24.89	0.45	23.70	3.77
1986	13.84	1.53	19.81	1.13

* Unadjusted CPI

Source: J. Teek and J. Wilcox, "A Real, Affordable Mortgage," *New England Economics Review* (January/February 1991), p. 51

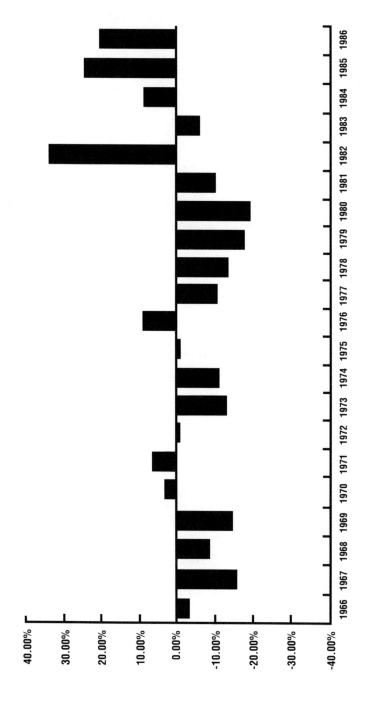

Figure 6.2. Change in Net Worth per Deposit Dollar* (1966–1986)

* Based on CTP Bank holding a portfolio consisting exclusively of long-term government debt.

the bank's worth per deposit dollar, if it had been in operation from 1966 to 1986 and if it had invested exclusively in seemingly prudent long-term government bonds. Figure 6.2 demonstrates that in 14 of the 21 years examined, the bank's net worth would have declined. Thus, the CTP Bank, with its unique structure of inflation-sensitive liabilities and contra-inflation-sensitive assets (if invested in long-term debt) would find its net worth subject to extreme fluctuations—both positive and negative. Of course, when the cumulative negative changes exceed the cumulative positive changes, the bank is insolvent.

The changes in net worth for portfolios consisting exclusively of common stocks, short-term government bonds, or long-term government bonds are shown in Table 6.3. There are large fluctuations for common stock portfolios; 9 of the 21 years show substantial losses. The short-term government portfolios would have resulted in 15 consecutive annual losses.

DEVELOPING REAL-RETURN FINANCIAL INSTRUMENTS TO HEDGE THE CTP BANK'S RISK

Because the CTP Bank's portfolio must provide returns at least equal to the inflation rate (its liabilities surely do so), the bank needs a hedge— long-term financial returns that promise to exceed the inflation rate. Such instruments have been developed and offered in limited amounts. The author has extensive experience in the development and practical implementation of these instruments and the problems they may entail.

Basically, the portfolio manager must locate highly rated issuers of long-term debt that would obligate themselves to issue inflation-corrected returns. Inflation-corrected financial instruments are often called real-rate or real-return instruments. A few such products now exist, including certificates of deposit (CDs) that are indexed to inflation and earn 3–4 percent above the inflation rate, some real-return bonds, and some real-return mortgages.

The entities that would be most likely to issue real-rate or inflation-adjusting financial instruments are producers whose revenues are highly sensitive to the price level—so that inflation tends to automatically increase the firm's revenues—and/or those whose assets appreciate systematically with inflation. Obvious examples are producers of relatively scarce natural resources. In fact, the prototype of all such natural resources, which has been thought of as the most reliable long-term inflation-beating store of value, is gold. However, being as "good as gold" has not been very good at

Figure 6.3. Price of Gold (1975–1991)

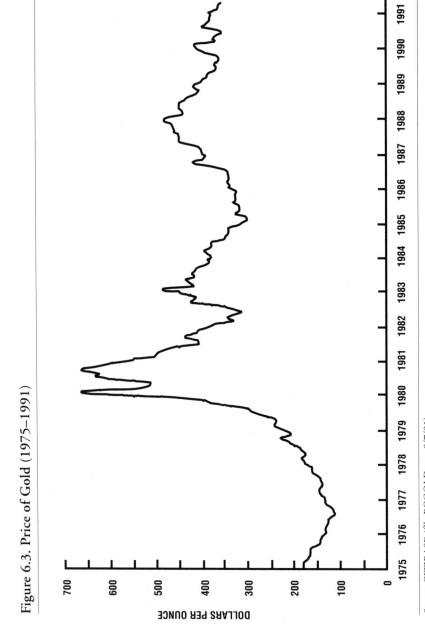

Source: CITIBASE (file PCGOLD rev. 8/7/91).

all over the past 15 years. As shown in Figure 6.3, recent gold prices have been about half those of the late 1970s. If gold had been a principal asset behind the CTP Bank's liabilities, the bank would have failed.

The lesson of gold should not be seen in isolation. A study of historical price booms for inelastically supplied natural resources examined prices of natural rubber after the wide adoption of rubber tires on automobiles between 1900 and 1910, industrial diamonds during the 1930s, and tin at the beginning of the twentieth century as extreme examples of raw material scarcity that would most likely result in long-term price appreciation.[6]

The common factor in each of these examples is that the price boom for these items, which surely exceeded overall inflation even for decades, set up a mechanism for the private market to ultimately respond with substitutes when the price of the "irreplaceable" became too high. When substitute natural resources were unsatisfactory, modern chemistry produced synthetic versions of rubber and industrial diamonds and developed a process that vastly reduced the demand for tin.

If scarce natural resources cannot reliably produce revenues that will exceed inflation, what about finished products such as automobiles? Although it is possible for the price of a product and its revenues to equal or exceed inflation for a period of time—appearing to make inflation-indexed liabilities possible—an individual firm is still subject to competition. A manufacturer with a declining market share would come to regret the day that it financed its long-term debt with inflation-sensitive obligations if the rate of inflation accelerated. The CTP Bank's portfolio manager would similarly regret purchasing such bonds, because the manufacturer's credit rating and the bond prices would drop well before the bonds were in default.

Another possible source of long-term inflation-adjusting debt is utilities, which need large amounts of capital requiring long-term debt financing. A utility might be confident that over the following decades it would be able to maintain its share of consumer and industrial spending, because in this industry competition is controlled. Accepting the inflation risk seems to be reasonable, except for the unknown of future utility rates set by politically sensitive boards and commissions. If utilities can rely on receiving inflation adjustments to their revenues, they become prime candidates for the issuance of inflation-adjusting financial instruments. In fact, a $300 million real-rate issue by a major utility was brought to market as a private offering.

Another group of possible issuers, with great potential to service inflation-sensitive obligations, is found in the real estate industry. This is true for the financing of both residential and commercial real estate. In either case, a particular variant of inflation-adjusting financing is necessary to make the inflation adjustment or the acceptance of the inflation risk palatable to the real estate borrower. One form of such inflation-adjusting financing that is manageable for the borrower, so as not to incur the shock of a sudden increase in inflation and the necessity to service a suddenly higher debt, is the price level adjusted mortgage (PLAM). The PLAM gives the borrower an incentive to accept the inflation risk by providing a low initial payment, which adjusts the payments so that the payment stream over time matches the level of prices in the overall economy.

For example, if inflation surges to 15 percent, most of the additional inflation interest due is tacked on to the balance of the mortgage, and the mortgagor amortizes the additional balance over the life of the mortgage, resulting in a smooth payment level. The mortgage is retired over its term, and the borrower—in return for a small initial debt service—agrees to accept the inflation risk by adjusting the level of regular payments to reflect the level of prices in the economy. With a 15 percent inflation rate, the payment level (not the rate) increases by 15 percent in the next time period.

In terms of the suitability of PLAMs to hedge the CTP's inflation problem—the size of the debt is important, and individual PLAMs should be transformed into mortgage-backed, inflation-adjusting bonds. This has been contemplated but not yet implemented.

PRACTICAL BARRIERS TO IMPLEMENTATION: A DIGRESSION

It is logical for MET and other state tuition plans to seek to acquire long-term, high-quality, inflation-adjusting financial instruments, and it might be financially advantageous for certain debt-issuing entities, such as commercial real estate operators or utilities, to finance a part of their operations with real-rate financial instruments; however, the issuance of such real-return instruments is hardly a foregone conclusion. Some writers have tried to explain why inflation-adjusting finance was a good idea that somehow had to be dismissed, due to some "mysterious" market barriers.[7] But when inflation-adjusting finance finally reached the market, it was proclaimed to be "a milestone in the history of this country's financial markets."[8]

The rationale for CTPs is risk shifting. Families want to shift the inflation risk to the CTP. By purchasing real-return instruments, the CTP, in turn, shifts the inflation risk to those entities that are equipped to handle it. The practical implementation of this process is difficult, but it can be done.

NOTES

1. See Paul M. Horvitz, "Is MET Insolvent? An Analysis of the Financial Performance of the Michigan Education Trust Under Bank Regulatory Accounting Principles," the College Savings Bank Research Division (November 20, 1990); Jeffrey S. Lehman, "Social Irresponsibility, Actuarial Assumptions, and Wealth Redistribution: Lessons About Public Policy from a Prepaid Tuition Program," *Michigan Law Review* 88 (April 1990).

2. The expected return differential between the MET plan and a self-investment program is influenced by the outcome of the efforts to shelter the MET's investment income from federal taxation, as well as the ability of the beneficiary to use individual retirement account (IRA) tax-free accumulations to fund tuitions.

3. Horvitz, "Is MET Insolvent?"

4. Eugene Kroch, "Tracking Inflation in the Service Sector," Federal Reserve Bank of New York, *Quarterly Review* 16 (Summer 1991).

5. In order to make allowance for the bank's operating expenses, its portfolio must grow at rates more rapid than its liabilities. The put discounts, on the other hand, reduce the required real return. The put discounts probably offset the expenses of the fund, so that the CTP's earnings must generally approximate the real tuition growth rate.

6. Stephen P. Magee and Norman I. Robins, "The Raw Material Product Cycle," in Lawrence Krause and Hugh Patrick, eds., *Mineral Resources in the Pacific Area* (San Francisco: Federal Reserve Bank of San Francisco, 1978), 30–55.

7. See, for example, Stuart E. Weiner, "Why Are so Few Financial Assets Indexed to Inflation?" Federal Reserve Bank of Kansas City, *Economic Review* (May 1983).

8. Zvi Bodie, "Inflation, Index-Linked Bonds, and Asset Allocation," *Journal of Portfolio Management* (Winter 1990).

9. Kit Lively, "Critics Hit Prepaid—Tuition Idea as Michigan Sees Its Surplus Decline," *Chronicle of Higher Education*, March 10, 1993, p. A32.

Index